The Three Trimesters of Prayer

Foreword by John Eckhardt

Melissa S. Sanders

All Rights Reserved. No part of this book may be reproduced or transmitted in any form or any manner, electronic of mechanical, including photocopying, recording or by any information storage and retrieval system, without permission in writing from the author/publisher. Please direct all inquiries to info@ellisandellisconsulting.org.

Published by:

Ellis & Ellis Consulting Group, LLC

www.ellisandellisconsulting.org

info@ellisandellisconsulting.org | 954-439-0760

Copyright © 2016 by Melissa S. Sanders

ISBN 13- 978-1539009313

10- 1539009319

Printed in the United States of America.

TABLE OF CONTENTS

	Acknowledgements	V
	Foreword	7
	Prologue	9
	Introduction	11
1	The First Trimester	29
2	The Second Trimester	53
3	Shift Your Posture and Prepare to Push	83
4	The Third Trimester	105
5	The Crowning of Purpose	129
	Endnotes	141
	About the Author	143

ACKNOWLEDGEMENTS

This book is dedicated to my Lord and savior Jesus Christ. Thank you for the strength, the courage and creative ability to articulate the living verbiage of a midwife, and to assist others in the Kingdom to produce after Your own kind.

Thanks for the encouragement, motivation, investments, and prayers of lifetime friends and family such as my mom, my best friend and brother for life (Jeremy of NC) and my god-mother who prayed consistently even through her own life challenges (Momma D. Ross).

To my covenant brothers and sisters (prayer partners) who encouraged me to be disciplined and consistent in prayer.

Cam (Birmingham) thanks for every prayer, conversation, and sacrifice of your time.

To my brother Will (NY/NC) who has been my prophetic IV, lifeline, and life coach through prayer and intercession. Grateful for times we pushed each other.

To the many churches, organizations, leaders, and the like that have and will continue to support this ministry, thank you. May our God continue to bless, preserve and propel you.

To **Apostle John Eckhardt** (Chicago, IL) – Thank you for being the strength, support, covering and resource that you are in my life. The foreword written for this book literally left me speechless. Thank you for believing in me!

FOREWORD

JOHN ECKHARDT

Best-Selling Author, Prayers that Rout Demons

Apostle, Crusaders Church (Chicago, IL)

There have been many books written on the subject of prayer. Many books are simply echoing what has been previously said. This book is different. **Melissa S. Sanders** gives a different perspective on prayer that is unique and revelatory.

Prayer is similar to being pregnant and bringing forth the plans and purposes of God. The danger of miscarrying, aborting, or giving your child up for adoption can be likened to the challenges of bringing forth the promises of God in prayer. Many believers have given up on prayer, and have not persisted until the birth and development of the dreams and visions of their heart. This book will encourage believers to press into prayer and see the glorious result of fulfillment in their lives.

This book will challenge you whether you are a beginner in prayer or more advanced. Melissa also discusses how the prophetic and apostolic anointing can influence our prayer lives. You can walk in more boldness and authority, and continue to grow and become stronger in this important area.

Melissa has a burden to see churches and believers walk in the power and strength of prayer. Her passion for this subject will come across on the pages of this book. I recommend this book to believers everywhere. Please consider and hear the truths in it, and receive the blessing of revelation. Consider what is said and may the LORD give you understanding in all things. (2 Timothy 2:7).

PROLOGUE

The general intercessor is no less than the apostolic intercessor.

The tunnel entry of this exploratory journey toward prophetic and biblical discovery opens the gates to fresh revelation, structure, strategy, and direction. As we stroll the grounds of prevailing prayer, we will walk through the blueprints as though it were a hidden fossil from the antiquated lands of an extinct wilderness. We will plow through the known and the unknown. It is my endeavor, through the unction of the Holy Ghost, that by the conclusion of your reading, comprehending, and studying you will birth the undiscovered you.

While many of you have been hidden, rejected, muzzled by the ox (1 Corinthians 9:9), and confused by the whimpering seed in your womb, the Lord was preparing a *midwife in waiting* to coach you through the delivery of power and greatness. This is the hour that those who have been impregnated with purpose and destiny shall bring forth (birth) a new sound of Kingdom authority and assurance. There is a guaranteed stamp of life on your seed that eradicates the possibility of abortion, miscarriage, and premature labor. The Father pre-birthed our purpose and destiny over 2,000 years ago when He gave His Son for us. Jesus travailed in pain and agony so that we could victoriously and perpetually produce in and for the Kingdom.

Isaiah 53:4 Surely he hath borne (birthed)

our griefs, and carried our sorrow;

Prior to this deep-sea dive, let me exterminate any insinuation of elitism. The descriptive trio, The Three Trimesters of Prayer, was in no way dissected in the sense of least to greatest. The general intercessor is no less than the apostolic intercessor. There are simply various roles, and as we discover our roles and take our positions on the walls of the spirit we will witness the greatest triumph of this time. Listen intently and posture yourselves to bear down as the weight of the Holy Spirit preps you for the **Three Trimesters of Prayer**.

INTRODUCTION

Know your seasons to fight, and know your seasons to rest!

Impregnated with the Burden of God

I am amazed to finally have the privilege of sharing my journey with you. Over the course of my life, I have been in the process of being constructed, reconstructed, and transformed into the full operation of a midwife, intercessor, and prophet. That is three trimesters in life alone! The five senses of the Spirit began to open up in every aspect of life from my childhood until now.

During many years of spiritual maturation, I found myself using terminologies I didn't understand after certain realms of prayer, such as "feeling open". I had no idea there was so much truth and reality to everything the Holy Ghost was introducing to me and birthing out of me. Examples such as this, and other mysteries of prayer, is what I want to define and identify for you as this journey continues.

This is primarily the entire purpose of this book. To speak to intercessors, prophets, and those who hear, see, and operate in the supernatural realm. That's a burden I will probably never lose; just to let you know you are not losing your mind. It has been quite an adventure to have to learn so much on my own.

That's why I count it an honor and privilege to be able to help the next generation, and perhaps the generation before me, to come to terms with the unique call of God on their lives. I believe that is the purpose of the call to midwifery. We don't stand out, or stand alone, without a purpose. We are responsible for each other's *accountability*. That's a word rarely used in the Body of Christ now. We must understand that in order to strive to the end we must utilize the prayers, strength, and testimonies of our fellow brothers and sisters.

Revelations 12:11 And they overcame him by the blood of the Lamb, and by the word of their testimony; and they loved not their lives unto the death.

By watching others there are some warfare strategies that we learn, and can often avoid, whether failed or successful. I truly believe I have gone through all that I have to help someone else. I'm not too proud to say to the next generation, *"Learn from my mistakes - learn what not to do."* Therefore, even my failures will serve a purpose and God still gets the glory out of my life. Guess what? Those naked ugly truths will be released here as well.

I would like to give a slight overview of the next several chapters in a nutshell, and then dissect each compartment of the book as we approach it. Let's deal with the overall setup. The Three Trimesters of Prayer explains the threefold process of intercession compared to the process of birthing a living seed. I am reluctant to use the word "levels" because, as stated in the abstract of the book, I do not want anyone to feel labeled as *more* or *less* due to their operation in prayer.

The reality is the warfare can very well be more intense predicated upon your targeted area. Visions may appear more. Perhaps one may have more mysterious, in-depth encounters in the spirit. Certain spiritual gifts and assignments coupled with laboring in prayer, such as the prophetic, can often determine the various manifestations in an intercessor's life. However, the point is that variety in operation does not make one more elite, or more important, than the other. It may simply mean one was introduced to another compartment (function or way) to transition in prayer differently than others.

In several areas you will see that I speak to apostles, prophets, pastors, teachers, and evangelists as well. Why? I believe it is impossible to walk in any function of the five-fold without being an intercessor, so the stories and advice also applies to the combined warfare of leaders and those in ministry. I am a prophet, so I will unconsciously refer to prophets in some segments.

To my fellow readers: Please be prepared and aware that just as messy and gross as it can be to watch a baby exit a woman's body, that's how intense some of the content may be as it relates to my testimony, my life, my process, and the things I have experienced as an intercessor and prophet in the making. I have cringed at the details and the level of transparency required of me. I have dreaded the warfare, persecution, and consequences for opening up about the truths of my life story. I can only pray that it reaches those God intends and saves lives. The ultimate goal of a Midwife is to save your seed by any means necessary.

The Trimesters of Prayer

Now as we enter into this dimension of teaching and fresh revelation let me give a brief discourse of the actual topic *The Three Trimesters of Prayer*. Throughout each process of prayer and ascension there are multiple births. Intercession is when you are burdened, or impregnated with the heart of God to pray His will in the earth. Depending on the situation, or the assignment, one can be unctioned to deliver what the Holy Spirit is praying through them, or receive a prayer request to bring before the Father.

Romans 8:26 - Likewise, the Spirit also helps our weakness: for we know not what we should pray for as we ought but the Spirit himself makes intercession for us with groanings which cannot be uttered.

Throughout the three trimesters we will also discuss in more detail the three postures of intercession as well as the pulls and weights (burdens) in the Spirit. Burdens often serve as an alarm in the spirit to travail and press, via prayer, the assignment for that moment or season.

Prayer Postures

In order to remain progressive in the process of birthing out prayer there are three postures. We will discuss each posture within the chapters in more detail.

Definition of General Intercession

a) **Impregnation** – the posture of impartation; receiving a deposit (instruction; burden; power) from the Lord.

Definition of Prophetic Intercession

b) **Incubation** – the posture of carrying the seed to full development; growing and maturing the gifts which are in us and assisting with the development of the Body of Christ through the edification of prophetic release and prayer.

Definition of Apostolic Intercession

c) **Manifestation/Delivery** - the posture of birthing out; bringing forth; setting order to; walking out vision and ministry through the strategies of prayer and intercession.

General Intercession

The Lord spoke to me years ago and partially defined the role of three types of intercessors. Even though there are more than three, these are the three focuses for this book. General Intercessors speak **to** God. Prophetic Intercessors speak **for** God. Apostolic Intercessors speak **as** God. I will give an example of each through biblical scenarios. David was a general intercessor in the Bible. Although David was one of the mightiest men mentioned; known as a warrior, he was consistently an intercessor.

He prayed from a place of brokenness, repentance, offered prayers of gratitude, prayers of petition, prayers for the nation, prayers for himself, and even prayers for his enemies. This is an example of a *true* intercessor. He is such a model for prayer he has many of his petitions written in what is known as the Book of Psalms. General intercessors, such as David, often pray about *every* single thing.

David was a man of war. His upbringing in his father Jesse's house was the foundational boot camp that prepared him for his battles with Goliath, the Amalekites, and even the Philistines. He was given the innate ability to fight and obtain guaranteed victories from the Lord over his enemies. However, while his experience and skill was insurmountable, he did not count it as his coverage and insurance, or perhaps his guaranteed victory. He invested his hope in God, not his ability. Though he was equipped, David still inquired of the Lord before battle. As a result, the Lord promised him that the victory would be given to him (1 Samuel 30:8).

The reason it is significant to hear, know, and follow the voice of God is because you must operate according to your trimester. What does that mean? Never attempt to carry, deliver, or operate on a level that you have not been dilated (stretched, trained, walked out in prayer). For example, if one is in their first trimester (stages) of becoming a runner, brisk walks would have to become strengthened prior to jogging, and jogging prior to sprints. Learn to strengthen your development by exhausting every level, extracting all knowledge, goods, strategies, and information out of each level of prayer.

Don't despise small beginnings (Zechariah 4:10). All too often, I see up and coming intercessors watching those with a microphone slicing through atmospheres like butter. They envy them. They want to leap out into the zones with them. They want to pray for people and see them fall out, and cast out demons because it looks powerful. It means the hymen of your pride has not been broken yet. You are still a virgin to the purpose of intercession when you crave the spotlight. There is no spotlight when you have experienced the warfare, the labor, the toiling, and the dark side of being an intercessor. The primary key to being an intercessor is to be invisible, selfless, and available for use as you fight on the backside.

It wasn't until recent years that being an intercessor, a gatekeeper, or a midwife even became popular. It has surfaced to the top with the rest of the "SHOWnanigans" that is taking place in the Body of Christ. It forces me to believe if the crushing that comes along with being an intercessor was truly being carried out, it would be far less people *proud* of the call. Again, just as a woman carrying a child, what she is carrying is beautiful, but the process is ugly and uncomfortable to her. Know your trimester. Study it. Sleep in it. Rest in it. Know each trimester inside out.

There was an instance where David inquired of the Lord regarding going to battle with the Philistines and the Lord told him not to fight this time. His instructions were to go up above the mulberry trees until he heard the sound of going (1 Chronicles 14:14). In this season David's instructions were to rest.

At certain points during a woman's pregnancy the physician tells her to come off of her job and stay off of her feet. Even during delivery women have moments when they tell her not to push. Just breathe. Even in the call for David to "go up", God often calls us up above and out of the second heaven (the place of spiritual battle) and out of places of warfare to rest and restore us.

There will be seasons that the Lord will give grace to bypass the second heaven. The grace to bypass the battles in the Spirit. The Lord also spoke that many have bypassed the trimester of bail-out. After one is so far along in their pregnancy they can no longer abort. You cannot quit because you are tired. You cannot quit because you are weary. Your promise is too far developed to pretend it doesn't exist. You already feel the kicks at this point. You already feel it moving. Press forth and release what is on the inside of you. It is Heaven's Best Investment.

The scriptures tells us ways to fight smarter and not harder. Decree verbal and biblical victories such as, *"The warfare is already accomplished in my life through Christ according to Isaiah 40:2."* If we follow His instructions, we often find the warfare is below us. What was once our ceilings become our floors.

Revelations 4:1 - Come up hither, and I will shew thee things which must be hereafter.

For example, during a woman's third trimester (I know it's too soon to discuss) she does not need to do anything strenuous. Her fight has already been hard enough just to make it through the first two. One must understand the seasons when God wants us to rest.

In order to handle the massive requests and unctions to pray, there must be a way to balance it all. Most intercessors are in constant prayer, battle, warfare, pressing, travailing and birthing. Know your seasons to fight, and know your seasons to rest! When I discovered I was called to intercession I denied it because I thought all intercessors prayed for three and four hours at a time. I didn't feel I had the stamina as much as I loved prayer. Yet I discovered God controls those moments. During those times I prayed as I was burdened (felt the weight of God) to do it. He knew how to tug on my spirit when there was a need for a specific situation, or matter at hand. I had to learn to trust Him with me!

However, the Lord was gracious to allow me to grow into those long hours of prayer. It began with an unusual love for Him. Not being able to get enough of His presence, His glory, and His power. In communing with Him, I started to feel greater weights and pulls to pray that seemed more urgent than they had before. I had to learn through much maturation the severity of those prayer unctions.

Note: Take every burden and unction to pray as a 911 call in the spirit. Never ignore the urge to pray!

Prophetic Intercession

Prophetic Intercession took quite a while to discover and realize it even existed. There were certain times when the Father summonsed me to prayer because an urgency was on the horizon in the spirit such as: sickness, death, warfare in the region, etc. Even before salvation, I could never understand why I knew kids were going to get shot in my school and feel the need to pray and warn them. In prophetic intercession it is much like prophesying through words of prayer. A great example, is being able to intercede via visions and dreams that are revealed. It is not the common operation that we experience during routine altar calls in corporate worship. It is not when we ask the individuals what they need prayer for and we pray accordingly.

Prophetic intercessors may be led to walk up to a person and say, "May I pray for you?" Upon that person's agreement, they may begin to travel in the spirit (allow the Holy Ghost to take them to the depth of a matter), and press beyond your flesh to pray for change in the matter revealed. This is a place where you may see a specific sickness, body part, or family member to pray for. After which they can confirm the prayer touched matters they never told anyone.

Other times prophetic intercessors may not know what to pray after having a specific vision or dream revealed. It may be a revelation released about an attack on the nation, the city, or perhaps your church. The Spirit makes intercession for you (Romans 8:26). This is when we speak **for** God. We pray what He prays through us. When I have dreams or visions about warnings or dangerous happenings that will take place in the world, I don't know the outcome. I have to trust my heavenly language to travel to the destination, or time of the event. That means it can be present or futuristic. Use your authority in God to decree and declare the outcome of the Almighty.

Many times there would be visions, dreams, etc. to help direct, with specificity, what to pray for. Moses is an example in the Bible of a prophetic intercessor. He went to the mountains to pray on behalf of the people, but he never came back empty handed. He came back with a "thus saith the Lord," a prophetic word of warning and even instruction for the people based on the deposit he received during visitations with the Lord.

Moses met with God on behalf of the people and came back to speak what the Father released to him. If the Father did not communicate directly with Moses he wouldn't know His plan to send destruction. If Moses did not feel the burden of the Lord and experience godly wrath because of the people's disobedience, he wouldn't have been able to intercept and shift what was about to take place. Why is this necessary? Because we are carriers!

Remember the definition that came with prophetic intercession? Most are in the posture of incubation. Webster defines incubation like so:

1) to keep (something) in the proper conditions for development;

2) to maintain (as an embryo or a chemically active system) under conditions favorable for hatching, development, or reaction;

We watch! We hear! We speak!

We sound the alarm to danger. We sound the alarm to the shifts and moves of God. We are the voices of penetration in our atmospheres. If you do not want change don't call us to pray in your church. If you do not want to shed normality and religion, then do not call us to be a part of your team. We are a great army and we represent a great God.

Just as prophets carry the secrets of God, so does the prophetic intercessor (Amos 3:7). We are God's conversationalists. It's hard to sit and listen to His heart and not act out of emotion! This is why intercessors must die to their emotions! If we allow our emotions to merge into our assignments, there are moments the condition, the fickleness, the carnality often seen in the Body of Christ will make you so angry you would welcome God's wrath. You will agree with Him to kill, or send destruction. However, that would defeat the purpose of being an intercessor.

No matter what type of intercessor you are, you must

intercept, to intercede. Be the go-between warrior even when you really want judgment to come. Moses smashed the Ten Commandments due to that very thing (Exodus 32:19). It is nothing like carrying the heart of God, and knowing the passion of the people. It is painful unto God and to the intercessor. It is what creates those burdens to wail before the Lord. It is the reason that many cry in services while others are rejoicing! The intercessors' pain is another person's rescue!

Intercessors must have strong, healthy wombs of compassion. This is why Jeremiah cried so much. He was as much an intercessor as he was a prophet. He had a lot of what I call "floor negotiations" with God. He spent time in prayer crying, begging, and pleading with God about His people, followed by prophetic rebukes to those who failed to work according to the system of God.

Jeremiah 23:1-2 (KJV) Woe be unto the pastors that destroy and scatter the sheep of my pasture! saith the LORD. 2Therefore thus saith the LORD God of Israel against the pastors that feed my people; Ye have scattered my flock, and driven them away, and have not visited them: behold, I will visit upon you the evil of your doings, saith the LORD.

Apostolic Intercession

Finally, I discovered there was an even stronger and more intense place of prayer called apostolic intercession. I'm sure some of you are thinking *Okay what are we going to have next, Hocus Pocus Intercession?* Believe it, or not, there is such a place of operation called apostolic prayer. I will explain in the upcoming chapters with more detail, but simply put – notice how Apostles build, establish, and set governmental order in the spirit? Well that's what apostolic intercessors do in prayer. Prophets and Apostles *say* what they see, whereas *prophetic* and *apostolic* intercessors *pray* what they see.

I'm sure many are wondering who the example could possibly be for an apostolic intercessor in the Bible. Nehemiah. Nehemiah had such a great task at hand he didn't even have time to really grieve. He got wind of the destruction that had taken place in Jerusalem. The Bible says he mourned for a few days, he cried, and he prayed, but then he got up and sought the Lord to rebuild (Nehemiah 2).

Even though he had the unction and approval of the Lord, the Bible does not say the Lord spoke the words to Nehemiah when he spoke to the people. Nehemiah was branded with apostolic instinct. He was already the cupbearer to the King. Part of his job was to sip of the King's drink before giving it to him. Just in case someone was trying to kill him, Nehemiah would take the hit. He gave him counsel and instruction. Do we understand the severity of being assigned to Kings? You are charged to lay your life on the line for those you serve.

Apostolic intercessors are often graced with positions in

high places and trusted by distinguished and illustrious individuals. They are the voices of instruction to Kings. Strategizing was in Nehemiah's blood. Without hesitation, without pausing to see what the verdict was and how many lives were lost, he immediately commenced to orchestrating a strategy for restoration. Not that the Lord didn't say it, but he had a relationship with the Father that was so cohesive he could express to the people how God would move and He did just that.

In Nehemiah 2:20 it says,

Then answered I them, and said unto them, The God of heaven, he will prosper us; therefore we his servants will arise and build.

He spoke with an authority as if he were God, not because he was *taking the place of God*. He spoke out of the confidence and posture of *knowing* his Father's thoughts. The phenomenal thing was that he knew the heartbeat of the Father and what He would, and would not say.

Do you see the pattern? There is so much diversity and uniqueness in the life of the intercessor. However, there are also great demands, mental drainage, and emotional pulls. If you haven't been teased for crying all the time, or feeling the presence of God and being pulled into prayer at the most inopportune times, or being considered *too much*...you might not be an intercessor. Intercessors are never NORMAL.

There were times I would leave the sanctuary or try to hide my face. Now I kneel before God, if possible without distraction, or simply lift my hands in prayer and worship to take in what the Father is saying while in the sanctuary. When He beckons us we must *lean in* and *lean close* to lend God our ear to hear Him speak. There is such a multiplicity of ways that we can operate as intercessors, but regardless of the difference, there is distinctiveness. We are all called to the vein of prayer wherein we are assigned for a purpose, and that purpose we shall discover.

One of the most unique things I learned was from an old intercessor, Dr. Doris Cooper Anthony of Montgomery, Alabama. The lesson was when an intercessor is moved by the spirit of God to cry and travail, it is not an embarrassment. She said, "It is a privilege for God to cry through us". That inspiration stays with me to this day. We must be willing and able to bear the burden of the country if God is requiring of us in prayer.

Again just like Nehemiah, after the tears there must be a great governmental authority as an apostolic intercessor. Let me warn you about something regarding the transition into apostolic intercession. Do not be alarmed if your emotions also dry up. Do you know why? Because strategy and sobriety is needed here. You will find yourself transitioning from praying in the prayer room to perhaps sitting on your deck with a notebook listening to the instructions of the Father.

Much maturity is needed in this place. It is time to begin raising up and developing other upcoming intercessors. This is when the Midwife in you must arise to help birth a nation of praying, intercepting voices to overthrow kingdoms and diabolical systems. It is the time to wake up and train on the existence of the 7 Mountains. These are the seven systems that surround us.

The Mountain of:
- **Business**
- **Government**
- **Family**
- **Media**
- **Religion**
- **Entertainment**
- **Education**

It is vital for you to know which mountain you are assigned to. It is vital that you know the mountain that possesses your wealth, health, and wholeness? As apostolic intercessors, we see ahead, we plan, strategize, and equip the people of God with biblical insight to obtain victory regardless of economic changes. It requires consistent insight through the mind of God and the brilliance of the Holy Spirit so that survival tools are mastered for our future.

Chapter One
The First Trimester: Impartation

"I'm Pregnant...Now What?"

General Intercession

S ay this out loud with me. "You cannot birth when there is no seed!" If you have natural children who remembers their first experience finding out they were pregnant? LOL! I am sure some laughed, cried, or wanted to kill somebody. Either way, your next question was, "What now?" If you picked up this book, you had some indication, or experience, that told you that you might be pregnant with intercession of some sort. You may not know the diversities of intercession. You may not know that your experiences in prayer can help you diagnose what kind of intercessor you are. Perhaps you may not be an intercessor at all. Many are asking, "What if I am just one who prays, but not called to intercession?"

Let's address the difference between prayer and intercession. The bible indicates a differentiation between both prayer and then intercession on several occasions. Please be clear from the onset. Anybody can pray what *they* desire to pray to God. Intercessors release through prayer what is "deposited" into their spirits by God. Intercessors cannot pray their will. An example of both would be:

1 Timothy 2:1 - I exhort therefore, that, first of all, supplications (requests), prayers (communication to God), intercessions (to stand between the problem and the answer), and giving of thanks (gratitude), be made for <u>all</u> men.

Another example, *Jeremiah 7:6 - Therefore pray not thou for this people, neither lift up a cry nor prayer for them, neither make intercession to me: for I will not hear thee.*

These are different approaches to prayer. For instance, if you are over the prayer or intercessory ministry at your local church, opening prayer cannot be approached the same way for every service, every atmosphere, and every situation. Some atmospheres and moments require us to war in the heavens. Some are more celebratory which only requires giving Him thanks. Some are lightly pressed, full of worship, and do not require a strong release at all. Others may require a bit more labor.

However, these varieties can only be discerned when there is an intercessor, or preferably, a team of intercessors created to monitor and discern, like the sons of Issachar, the times and the seasons (1Chronicles 12:32).

Romans 8:27 And he that searcheth the hearts knoweth what is the mind of the Spirit, because he maketh intercession for the saints according to the will of God.

To monitor the times and seasons means one must first be sensitive to the Father, be able to discern an atmosphere, and shift the posture and approach based on what God is requiring. Be flexible. How do you do that? Operate in the season of God. We commune with Him to hear His heart and what He desires to be released into the earth, as well as in our home or sanctuaries. Those who simply pray, release prayers from the earth realm (flesh realm) up. It is prayer based on the reality of the problem. It is prayer based on what one's emotions tell them to pray because they are not receiving from the Holy Spirit instructional prayer. They are simply releasing their heart to the Father. That is fine. That is all that is required to pray, but not for an intercessor.

When someone is very ill or at the point of death, you often hear people saying things like, "Lord just let your will be done...they may be better off with you." Not that we don't know God's will is going to be done regardless, but as intercessors we don't pray from a defeated place. We speak with authority and we speak with the voice of faith until the matter turns otherwise.

Intercessors leave the earth realm and pray from the heavens down. We want our prayers to reflect and echo the heart of God. We also want to exercise authority and boldness in our decrees. Therefore, we have been instructed to pray along these lines, "*Our Father which art in heaven, Hallowed be thy name. Thy kingdom come, Thy will be done in earth, as it is in heaven* (Matthew 6:9-10)." The Bible says in Luke 18:1 "*...men ought to always pray and not faint.*" Prayer is a corporate command in the earth for all, just like praise, "Let everything that has breath praise the Lord" – Psalm 150.

Yet there are times many specifically feel, hear, and carry the burden of the Lord. Intercessors, don't become uneasy when you can't pray in your natural language, but the spirit thrusts you to pray in your heavenly language. Intercession keeps us from praying our will. Intercession takes over when we don't know what to pray as we ought to (Romans 8:26). Stop fighting those moments when the Holy Ghost is shifting your dialect and your direction of prayer.

There will be times the burden will get so heavy, that just as a woman going in labor there is a magnetic pull to the floor. It is God's command for you to lay prostrate before Him. Often times you may see certain people come to the altar during worship service. If you are reading this book, more than likely you are one of the ones pulled to the altar. It does not mean you are trying to be deep, or seen, but there is something the Father wants poured out in that moment.

You want to stand up, but you can't. You want to be quiet,

but you can't. You want to act or be normal, not cry, not travail, but the weight of the Father's heart is coming through and you must bear down and push. Push until your will is out of the way and the purpose of the Lord prevails through you (Proverbs 19:21).

General Intercession: What to Expect

What is general intercession? It is a limitless availability and sensitivity to be on-call as a watchman in the earth. These are intercessors who often deal with foundational matters such as Church issues, special prayer requests, etc. It is the posture to stand in faith and release petitions up to the Father on another's behalf. If someone asks them to pray for a family member, they pick up the burden and pray right then, if not when they get to their designated places of prayer.

They can place a list of names in their Bible, such as the sick and shut in, and cover them in prayer effortlessly. Their prayers often last for hours because of the expansive areas that are covered on a consistent basis. Therefore, you can say they *Pray what they receive.* They pray what they are impregnated with, the need for God to come on the scene. Pretty broad right?

General intercessors often pray based on the information, prayer requests, and direction given. They also pray, by nature, just to be close to God. It was years during my life of prayer that I realized it was my calling to intercession that made me so different and hungry for God all along. I didn't know it was not normal, or it was not common amongst all people to desire to lay out in prayer for 3 to 4 hours a day. I was also very critical of others if they did not want to pray as long as I did, until I realized that was my charge and it was a grace given to intercessors.

Having diagnosed this reality, though still challenging at times, it helped me to become more comfortable with my spiritual differences from others. No, everyone might not understand when I have to get up and leave a dinner gathering, or the church picnic, because the Lord is calling me to prayer or to intercede for someone. We have to be okay with the voluntary employment of being *On-Call* for God 24/7. Some are probably asking, "When did I sign up *voluntarily* for this?" That's easy. When you told God, "YES!"

Think about it from a natural perspective. Those who are first responders and work for 911 dispatch know all too well how important it is to be there for the emergency. Answering that call and getting the call through to the emergency team can mean life or death for someone. It is just that severe in prayer! How fast we put the call through to God, dispatch the angels, and send help can mean life or death to a situation.

The posture of general intercessors is to be open to impregnation. Why? You cannot birth that which has not yet impregnated you. Let's go in depth. Most general intercessors have an overall passion for prayer. There is often no specificity to their direction. You need an injection of God's heart and His Word for the arousal of prayer to even begin.

Let's dissect Psalm 37:4 really quick. "Delight yourself also in the LORD; and he shall give you the desires of your heart." Most will take that as God will give you whatever you want to have. In retrospect, as intercessors spending time with Him causes a heart exchange. He will give us His heart and make it the desires of our heart.

Most often, general intercession is the place many intercessors get started before transitioning, or identifying, the specificity of their intercession; their type of intercession. Before I discovered I was called to prophetic and apostolic operation, I simply felt the need to pray, worship, or commune with God without needing anything other than Him.

I couldn't seem to get enough of prayer, His presence, His glory growing up. Before I knew I was called to preach, I was called to intercession. Before I knew I was called to be a prophet, I was called to intercession. Many times, intercessors, you won't know what to pray. When the Lord first begins His courtship with you, He woos you. He captures your heart. Many begin to feel a tugging they can't explain. Some just begin to pray in tongues with seemingly no direction (Jude1:20; Romans 8:26). Trust me! It's targeting something, even in you.

You just don't know what.

Remember when you first started dating? The conversation could have been about absolutely nothing, but you would just sit on the phone and listen to the other person breathe. You listened to stories about their life, their goals, their dreams, what attracted them to you and you to them. It is the process of getting to know them. Perhaps you became intimate at some point afterwards, whether you should have or not. The point I am making is you had to get close in order to consummate. Once you consummate it opens the opportunity to impregnate.

Go with the shifts of God until something is specifically revealed that you can begin to target. Pray for everything under the sun. Release that pressure. Let your water break in the spirit. When I was maturing in this I took the scripture literally from 1Thessalonians 5:17 *"Pray without ceasing."*

There will be days you won't know why you feel the need to pray. As mentioned in the intro, you often feel this weird turning in your belly. Sometimes you feel like crying, nervousness, confusion...just all sorts of emotions. You are not crazy. You will hear me release that a lot to keep it at the forefront of your mind.

Even at the ripe age of 14 years old, I would often find myself in the midst of having fun with friends, watching a movie, and that pressure would hit my belly. It often felt like what I called "surges" or "shocks." Many times it would be followed by trembles, or the shaking of the Lord's presence, indicating urgency and severity. There was a moment the spirit of God shook me all night, and in prayer through tongues all I could make out was, "New Zealand. A shaking in New Zealand." I knew that meant an earthquake. I kept praying. Three days after an earthquake hit New Zealand, but was light. I believe the Father impressed upon me to pray, or it could have been worse. Do you see why we can't brush off His commands to pray?

I would quickly have to excuse myself to an empty room, or closet, to release the burden of what was being dropped on me in prayer. Some might say, "*Oh it's not that serious. Some people are so heavenly minded they are no earthly good.*" God uses five blessings He gave us called senses. It is our way of communicating in the natural, why not in the Spirit?

When there's something major coming up, it is common to get butterflies in our stomachs right? As intercessors and prophets, we have to trust our senses (signs) in the Spirit. Our bellies turn just the same, and so if we don't keep our eyes lifted and our spirits ascended in heavenly places there may be no warnings or alarms released in the earth to the people (Ezekiel 33) who are not graced to hear God before trouble arises. Our wombs are God's alarm clocks in the earth.

A few other traits I've heard mentioned, and even experienced myself are 1) burning ears as God is speaking, 2) visions, 3) smelling certain things, 4) hands or other areas of one's body burning which relates to touch, and of course 5) taste. All of these are ways God deals with intercessors about what to pray. He uses what He gave us to speak to and through us.

The Bible says in Luke 18:1 *"...men ought to always pray and not faint."* *"Pray without ceasing,"* 1Thessalonians 5:17. Intercession is like a newborn baby that does not know the difference between night and day yet. It will wake you up at 3:00a.m. tossing and leaping in your spirit to break free, and just the same it will stir your belly in the middle of the day while trying to work or attend to your daily duties.

In a hilarious way, intercession can be a little rude. It does not mind weaving into a conversation and shifting your language into tongues while you may be trying to tell a funny joke, or talk about the latest changes of your kids...without your permission! It just jumps in where it fits in.

If you are like me, your friends may ask you how it is possible to shift from laughing to speaking in tongues in 2.2 seconds. It is the Holy Spirit's way of saying, *This is not the time to joke and play. I need you alert. Something is about to happen.* Intercession is a 24/7 job. I am not saying you have to walk around speaking in tongues all day, but you must be alert and on-call. Intercessors can't be so far off into carnality and fulfilling the lusts of your flesh that you miss the call of the

Father when He needs you. We must always scoot our will, our plans, and our agendas to the side and make way for the purpose of God to prevail (Proverbs 19:21).

However, there is a purification and discipline required in the spirit when it comes to intercession, just like there is a purification and discipline required in the spirit when it comes to worship.

John 4:24 - They that worship Him must worship Him in spirit and in truth.

Adapting to Intercession: Is This Normal?

Everyone does not avail themselves and purify themselves to press into the dimensions of prayer that can be effective for the matters at hand. Intercessors shouldn't have to be asked to pray, because they should always be in prayer mode. They shouldn't have to gear up and gird up to pray because they should wear the garments, the mantles of prayer. People who are used to common/commercial prayer can get up five minutes before service starts, put something religious in the atmosphere and keep it moving.

Have you ever walked into your church on Sunday mornings ready to lay at the altar expecting others to follow? Only to see people laughing, talking, chewing gum, and it vexed you to tears? As an intercessor, you can feel what the Lord DESIRES to do, but you have to figure out how to: 1) bring your flesh under subjection, 2) not see the actions and faces of the people, and 3) pray that the purpose of the Lord prevails (Proverbs 19:21).

Unless we are one with Him and in sync with Him, our concept of things will often be totally different from the function of God. As intercessors, we thrive on thinking with His mind, feeling with His heart, and moving with the winds of God. For example, it is a biblical command that we "*Enter into His gates with thanksgiving, and enter His courts with praise,*" according to Psalms 100:4. However, that is simply the basic principles of entering into the temple of God. It is a commanded routine that is often made unconsciously religious.

Nevertheless, when an intercessor enters in knowing the purpose of the Lord, the approach to prayer changes. The Lord may be angry with His people because of iniquity and sin, yet the congregation still attempts to *enter into His gates with thanksgiving.* It smells foul in the nostrils of God and grieves the heart of the intercessor. The true intercessors cannot ignore that and pray an exciting prayer – ignoring the stench in the room.

Unfortunately, today the forced commands of charisma, excellence, and timed-services tie the hands of liberty and freedom in most aggregations. The intercessor is often found muzzled, outnumbered, and rushed off to the side for the next moment of excitement on the program to proceed. The burden does not lift and the Father has not forgotten what He's revealed to the intercessor. Therefore, they are left feeling the pressure of disobedience to God, or obedience to the set authority of that ministry.

As I mentioned earlier regarding those over intercessory teams and ministries, I really want to help you deal with your frustrations in this book! I will release personal testimonies from my experiences, mistakes, and challenges as an intercessor that will prayerfully bring clarity and understanding. All of them won't be good stories, but I believe many will be able to relate, correct their posture, and save their seed.

Beware! Those frustrations come to cause you to abort within the first trimester of really discovering what is on the inside of you. As it is with natural pregnancy, you only have so long within the beginning stages to abort. The enemy attempts to cause you to stop what is on the inside of you before it can ever really get started. Many adolescents in the spirit often approach me or ask questions about what they are starting to experience in prayer, but they are new and clueless to the things that will try to come to shut them down or make them second guess their gifts.

Their innocence and love for God is often tainted by wicked, religious, controlling voices that will express, "There is no such thing as speaking in tongues. Being too deep will drive you crazy." They will even abuse scripture and ask if Jesus ever spoke in tongues. Never stop the growth and development of your seed. It will feel abnormal at first, especially when you are looking for a multitude of others to feel the same thing. This is why you are specifically called to intercession. To cry out against and beyond the norm.

As intercessors, you will walk the floor and labor with the discomforts of your seed. It is normal for you to pick up the uncomfortable kicks in the atmosphere that is not like God such as: the need for purification and repentance, the progressiveness of your church, or making sure your leaders are properly "gated" in prayer.

I ministered at a church once and I saw a picket fence around the entire sanctuary with gaps in it. The Lord pressed upon me to tell the intercessors to close in the gaps with prayer. The house was open for attacks due to the lack of *effective* intercession. I believe they were a praying people, but there was such a religious, antiquated stagnancy present. A lot of critical areas were uncovered.

It brings about a God-induced wailing, burden, and heaviness in your spirit to see these things because breakthrough and warfare is having a fight. Change and stagnancy were butting heads.

Ephesians 6:12 For we wrestle not against flesh and blood, but against principalities, against powers, against the rulers of the darkness of this world, against spiritual wickedness in high places.

There is much warfare in the Church regarding prayer, intercession, glory filled atmospheres, and the lack thereof. The deeper you journey into intercession, the more your senses and awareness will pick up. It is the Father's desire that our atmospheres be so ignited with His Spirit that the drug users, alcoholics, prostitutes, homosexuals and the like, will come into our services and be arrested by God's power.

Not because we took oil, slapped a cross on their forehead, and waited for them to sizzle like a demon in a horror film. God's love is precious, and we aren't praying or fighting to push something through that He does not already want to release. He desires to blanket us with Glory so heavy that it removes the focus off of the people and what we want to do. That upsets the spirit of pride and religion, because it makes flesh invisible. Flesh wants to be seen, acknowledged, and reverenced. It must die!

However, preparation is required. It is often baffling to intercessors to understand why it is so hard to get other Christians to pray more. Fast more. Seek God more. Why don't they want to labor and dwell in the presence of God? The intercessor cries their heart out, not understanding that the burden of prayer is the gift to hurt on behalf of others. We've just been graced and chosen for the job. We desire for them, what they don't know to desire for themselves.

Bonding with the Seed in Me

As expected, a first-time mother will begin to dive into a sea of books, magazines, pamphlets, and take on all the knowledge she can. It is her desire to know how she can be the perfect mother and what she needs to do in order to birth a healthy baby. Most call it *Bonding with Baby*.

Spiritually this means the pulls, the turnings in your belly, the yearning to cry out before God will not go away. Get used to bonding with the presence of God. Wrap your mind around the fact that you do not have a schedule when it comes to prayer. It will wake you in the midnight hour. You must answer the call.

There were nights that I would feel the power of God in my sleep and would hear the tongues rolling out of my mouth and tried to shake it and turn over and fluff my pillow, but the discomforts and the kicks of intercession would wake me in the wee hours of the morning much like a pregnant woman who cannot get comfortable, who wakes for a midnight snack. Intercessors your midnight snack is God. Your midnight snack is feeding on His presence. Your midnight snack is communion with the Father of your seed.

You must realize this is a part of you. It grows up in you. Again, as a child I could never get enough of God. It was most common for Pentecostal kids to do what we called *playing church*. We mocked all of the church members' praises. We quoted their testimonies verbatim and we'd take turns ushering one another and falling out on the playground. However, for some reason when the moment was over for the other kids I still wanted that moment to last. Although from the outside it appeared we were just playing church, deep down inside I wanted something to break out and happen for real.

I would come home from church some days as young as 8 years old and go into a room alone and pray that God would **do it to me,** meaning whatever He'd **done to** the shaking, shouting, screaming saints I'd witnessed in the sanctuary. When I did not get the response I thought that I would receive from God, I pouted and was hurt because I wanted to know why He would not touch me like He did the people at church. I had enough sense to know it wasn't normal for an 8-year-old to spend hours asking for God's presence when I could have been asking for dolls or toys, and I told Him so. When I did play with dolls I played church with them all day long!

What I did not recognize was my character and spiritual instincts had already kicked in even at that early age. A more relevant identification to my behavior probably should have been make-believe instead of *playing church*. As children, most *make themselves believe* in their dream world and in their personal fantasies. My dream was to be filled with the Holy Ghost and used mightily by God. I'm sure God laughed at me saying, "*My child, you have soon enough to deal with all I am going to release upon you in the years to come. Enjoy life while you can.*" If I had known what my future really held, I would have been as patient as possible.

I officially gave my life to the Lord and was baptized at the age of 14 and immediately began seeing visions and journaling things I'd heard from God. Yet no matter how much I saw, experienced, or felt it wasn't enough. As I grew older I discovered much more than intercession of course, but it was the vehicle of intercession that drove me into the awareness of other gifts such as preaching, laying hands, and prophesying.

Singing was the foundation of all my gifts, and it was so weird how my gifts began to interact with one another. I learned to sing in the spirit, or sing in tongues, without anyone telling me. My sounds changed and began to develop into melodies I did not hear in the traditional church. This was possibly around the age of 15. One gift merged into another. Yet, during every experience I birthed prayer even the more. What I discovered was the foundation of my hunger was to be close to God. Just as it is a newborn's instinct to reach for the mother's breast for feeding so it is the nature of one called to intercession to suck from the breastplate of righteousness.

As we seek for Him, the womb of our intercession expands. How? Remember those frustrations we talked about? When starting out as a new intercessor you don't have to try to extend thirty minutes of prayer into two hours. By the time issues and concerns continue to hit your spirit, it will extend! Go with the flow of your development.

The intercessor in us becomes pregnant with gifts. Our gifts become pregnant with purpose. Our purpose becomes pregnant with destiny until ultimately we are pregnant by Him, through Him, and with Him. All the while we are on a lifelong journey to birth Manifestation. The key factor becomes Birthing God in the Earth. How do we birth God in the earth? We birth His will! We become Him, little gods in the earth. What He speaks, we pray, and we become.

John 10:34(NIV) Jesus answered them, "Is it not written in your Law, 'I have said you are "gods"?

By this, we begin to take on the nature of God, the heart of God, the tears of God, the wrath of God, and the joy of God. How can we pray His heart if we do not know or feel His heart?

Isaiah 55:8-9 *"For my thoughts are not your thoughts, neither are your ways my ways, declares the* Lord. *As the heavens are higher than the earth, so are my ways higher than your ways and my thoughts than your thoughts."*

We take on the Five Senses of Christ. As the chapter title states, *I'm Pregnant...Now What?* Now that I know I am an intercessor, what do I do? Now that the burdens of the Lord have started to fall, what do we do? How do we get a release? How do we remain in order during church services when the travail of the Lord is dilating and pressing the womb of our spirits to be birthed out? What happens when the valves of prayer close up within the church or leader? As we deal with the three postures of each trimester, many of these questions will yield answers by way of the Holy Ghost; transparent answers we may not want to hear. It requires selflessness.

First and foremost, eat the Word! Digest the Word! Birth the Word! Pray the Word! There will be a lot of spiritual and prophetic terminologies and jargon used in this book, because I am more of a poetic expressionist. However, prayer should be laced with the Word of God to ensure guaranteed results. God's Word never returns void (Isaiah 55:11). What does that mean? His Word will never be sent out without accomplishing results.

Follow the Doctor's Orders

One of the things that is quickly discovered in the maturing stages of intercession is that the Lord will test your obedience and your faith. When a woman is pregnant, she may feel like she is strong enough to work until her water breaks. She may feel like she can take on the world despite this ever-changing mechanism in her body. Yet her physician will often tell her otherwise. Some are placed on bed rest due to possible complications. Others are told to become a little more active to keep their heart rate up, or to make sure they don't have a lazy labor, where it takes the baby forever to come during delivery.

Regardless of your trimester (the growth of your intercession) it is vital that Faith remains as your foundation of development. Obedience becomes the legs of your faith. You must follow the Doctor's (God's) orders. The Lord cannot trust life and death situations in your hands, if you are still fumbling over whether you really heard God, or not. What most beginner intercessors wrestle over most is if they really heard God. Guess what? Prayer can never be wrong.

Don't be found wrestling with your will. When the doctor says, "Mrs. Cantaloupe you gained 20 lbs. in a month and that just cannot continue. This is your new diet until the baby gets here." If the doctor tells her the risk she is facing and she continues in her process not adhering to it, she faces the risk of harming herself as well as what she is carrying. Embrace this question *What is the Greater Loss?*

If God says to pray for someone for an hour and it's 4:00 in the morning, is the greater loss to ignore the pull to get maybe two more hours of sleep? Is the greater loss to find out five hours later that the person died in their sleep, or committed suicide? Most of the time the things we wrestle and battle over are not worth the fight. Just do it. It is simply the warring of our members (flesh). Just obey God!

In the first trimester, the Lord is often lenient with us as we become acquainted with the change of life, the change of becoming a new spiritual parent and the various patterns and shifts that this journey introduces to us. As we deal with the process of progressing towards prophetic intercession, let me emphasize that it is the intercourse of prayer, worship, and intimacy with the Father that stretches our womb. It impregnates us with multiple assignments (purpose) and creates multiple births (manifestation of His will). In the natural, the more a person has sexual intercourse the more likely they are to become pregnant. Right?

The more time we spend in prayer and communicate with God, the more likely He is to release the seed (His will) for our lives. Life is centered around getting closer to God. We just want to spend time with Him and get to know Him better. The intimacy of prayer is initially appeasing to our flesh. The *feel-good moments* of being introduced to His presence, chills down our spine, and the warmth of His glorious touch will keep us in prayer for hours at a time. Let's not forget the climaxing relief of self-indulged prayers, the cumbersome release of our problems to Him. Don't we just love prayer as long as we are getting something out of it?

Yet very few are equipped to handle the responsibility of the deposit, being Parents of Intercession! Many are not mature and responsible enough to get up at 3:00am to feed a hungry seed of intercession, just as one has to feed a whimpering newborn. As any mother will tell you, it is no longer about you. Very few are willing to go through the humiliation, rejection, brokenness, purification, and pain only for your reward to be, "I pleased the Father."

I hear the Lord saying even in this moment, *"Because you didn't seek to be big, high, mighty, or deep in the sense of elitism, I will use you. I will call you. I will work miracles, signs, and wonders through your dedication to prayer."* It is in this place that you feel the accelerating pulls of intercession into higher heights and deeper depths of God (Ephesians 3:18).

> Psalm 42:7 - *Now the deep calleth unto the deep.*

Your ears draw closer to His lips. The mind of God is then migrated into the mind of those who have merged their thoughts with His by thinking what He thinks, speaking what He speaks, doing what He does, and shifting as He shifts. You are maturing, growing, and it shows. You are preparing for your second trimester.

Chapter Two
The Second Trimester: Incubation
Prophetic Intercession

"Discovering the Shifts, Moves, and Development of Your Seed"

The second trimester can be a bed of roses one minute and an absolute monster the next. It is all in how you mature, go with the flow of change, and develop your strength for the trimester (season) you are in. I would like to think this should be one of the most exciting times during your pregnancy. By now, you are starting to show your baby bump. Your baby is kicking and moving. You are feeling things you have never felt before. You are probably more emotional. Your mind is going a million miles a minute trying to imagine the future of your new baby.

From a spiritual aspect, everything about you is starting to change. A new side of your spirit is starting to emerge and others are noticing too. Your prayers no longer sound surface, or general. You may have started to take on a new dialect, or shift in tongues during prayer. Believe it or not, many who have been praying for years did not know one can actually pray a language in tongues. In the book of Acts, when they were filled with the Holy Ghost the bible says, *"Now when this was noised abroad, the multitude came together, and were confounded, because that every man heard them speak in his own language* (Acts 2:4)." Praying in your heavenly language, tongues, also builds and edifies your spirit man (1Corinthians 14:4).

Now you are learning to pray what you hear and flow in the spirit and not just the matter at hand. Prayerfully your natural emotions are coming under control, but spiritually you have become more sensitive – perhaps crying more during church services, quickening and being shaken by the spirit of God as you are carrying the shifts of the spirit in your belly. Just as a natural baby, know that what is in you is living, breathing, and growing. Just as many pregnant mothers become super sensitive and emotional, it is the same for an intercessor.

Did you know in the natural during the 16th – 20th week of pregnancy when you start to feel your baby move it is called "quickening"?[1] Well that is what happens in our spirit man when the Lord releases a Word or revelation to us. The power of His Word quickens us. It is moving us from where we are and closer to our destiny.

Romans 8:11 "But if the Spirit of him that raised up Jesus from the dead dwell in you, he that raised up Christ from the dead shall also quicken your mortal bodies by his Spirit that dwelleth in you."

That word quicken comes from the Hebrew word *chayah*[2],

which means to *come alive*! It is the moment of revelation, interpretation, and understanding of the mysteries of God's Word. Have you ever been reading the Bible and had an *Aha!* moment? It is because the Spirit of the Lord has been made alive in you, and what was once a mystery (unknown) to you is now revealed and unfolded.

Luke 8:10 - And he said, unto you it is given to know the mysteries of the kingdom of God: but to others in parables; that seeing they might not see, and hearing they might not understand.

There is a reason others don't feel what you feel in the spirit. There is a reason that you can try to explain the encounters, the visions, the constant burdens of prayer and others look at you strangely, even some leaders. Become comfortable with the idea that many just will not understand your process as, first...an intercessor, then most definitely not a prophetic intercessor. Prophetic intercessors often take on many of the same likenesses and experiences as prophets, not to be confused with walking in the office of a prophet.

Those who are of the Pentecostal persuasion are quite familiar with the term *quickening*. It was nothing like the old mothers that would quicken and holler out during service when the spirit of the Lord moved them. (Chuckling at the memory) Well in that same instance sometimes one's physical body can jerk under the power of God's release just as the movement of a baby is defined as quickening (jerking). Typically, a baby jerks because it has not yet learned to control the limbs and movements of its body as a newborn.

As a prophetic intercessor, your focus should never be rallied around learning to *control* anything. The whole idea and challenge in being an intercessor is to be flexible, available, and willing to be used in anyway God sees fit. That may be inclusive of moments that can make you look foolish, humiliated, or out of order to the natural eye. I am not excusing adolescent mindsets for those *choosing* to be out of order in corporate worship settings. Neither am I condoning the lack of teaching and understanding. However, as we mature in our prophetic understanding, or our wisdom of how to function under the anointing in various atmospheres, we don't become so learned or analytical that we can't remain what I call *limp* in His presence. Lose the resistance! Shift with God and always be flexible to His commands.

When something is limp, it can bend whichever way our hands direct it. A noodle must become wet, or boiled, to become chewable. To become limp in Christ we become so saturated in prayer and in His presence, that however He chooses to throw us, send us, direct us, speak to us we are willing and obedient.

Isaiah 1:19-20 If ye be willing and obedient, ye shall eat the good of the land: But if ye refuse and rebel, ye shall be devoured with the sword: for the mouth of the Lord hath spoken it.

Our womb is controlled by Him. Our words are controlled by Him. Our prayers are controlled by Him. You become limitless regarding where He carries you. You are open to soar through even some of the scariest places, i.e. the second dimension, where you are having to fight the prince of the air, spiritual wickedness in high places, rulers of the darkness of this world, etc. (Ephesians 6:12). Trust that He is your guide, your sword, your protector.

Here we learn the power of our hands, our mannerisms, and our gestures as a prophetic intercessor. Any skill, or piece of knowledge, downloaded by the power of the Holy Spirit is a resource to be used. Remember this. Never doubt what you did not have the mental capacity to come up with anyway. It is the brilliance of the Holy Ghost that gives us what to do and when to do it. Many refer to it as being over the top, too deep, or down right crazy because you may find your hands shooting out in a war-like manner in the atmosphere during prayer or in church. Chopping, swaying, pointing, slicing, etc. are often hand movements that the Holy Spirit performs, not you. David said, "Lord teach my hands to war and my fingers to fight (Psalm 144:1)."

David was a literal warrior and because he often had no

idea what he was coming up against he had to ask God to train him since it was the Lord who allowed him to take on the battles. When we hit certain dimensions and spiritual realms we encounter visions, shifts, and warfare that we had no idea existed. We must decree victory according to the Word of God. He encourages us with a declaration through His word that says in Isaiah 40:2 *The warfare is already accomplished.* It takes the leading of the Lord in our prayer languages, in our hands, and sometimes even with prophetic motions of our bodies to eradicate the evil manifestations in the earth that our natural eyes cannot see.

Ezekiel 4:4 - "Then lie on your left side and put the sin of the house of Israel upon yourself. You are to bear their sin for the number of days you lie on your side.

Do not allow your fear, opinions from others, or other reservations to hinder your training from the Holy Spirit. As many will find during their walk, the spirit of God may be your only source of training until He sees fit to send you help. You must trust His leading, His guidance, and divine credentials.

Midwives and Mentors

The most critical discovery during this trimester is, *who has become your physician in the earth?* Life, growth, and process has taught me a valuable lesson. Not everyone can be your physician. Not everyone can speak into your life, or even give advice concerning what you are carrying if they have never carried it. There's nothing worse than receiving a prescription given for symptoms you are not having. Better yet, a prescription being given to you that is not applicable to symptoms you *do* have. Who takes Pepto-Bismol for a headache? It is an erroneous diagnosis and in some cases and even more critical treatment.

That is how prophetic people and intercessors often feel when trying to explain their burdens. Be careful about receiving a diagnosis from someone without expertise on the specificity of your seed. Don't get frustrated when the advice from those you submit to seem to hit a brick wall. Don't get upset when training is refused. They cannot train what they can't diagnose! Your posture is still to submit, pray, and obey. **God honors honor!** You need a prophetic sonographer! Should the Lord be gracious and send you a Midwife, be ever so grateful! Especially a prophetic midwife - one who understands the process of birthing, and can see what you are carrying before you can! Someone to coach you through your adolescent stages and will help mature you, stretch you, and prep you for delivery.

When my spiritual father first birthed me into prayer, it was like me nursing from the breast of my mother. She produced the milk, all I had to do was lay there and feed from her. He produced such an atmosphere of prayer, praise, and worship until many of us under his ministry became greedy and spoiled at times. However, it introduced me to the taste and the flavor of prayer. I began to develop a craving for spending time with God. He taught us to *practice the presence of God.*

We were a prophetic and apostolic ministry that was never dry, religious, or lifeless. What burdened him, burdened us. It was a prophetic house, so the house was pregnant with the same purpose! It was a mighty training ground for much of my current operation in prayer. We lived off slogans like, *"We might as well go hard, or go home!"* He would call prayer at midnight, 5:00am, on weekends. Yet each time, there was a mandate for the services to be full of power and fervor, no matter who led the prayer. There was a demand placed on our wombs to birth the will and heart of God.

We developed an expectation for the supernatural because that is the place that we lived, breathed, and had our being. I longed for the anointing that was upon this man's life. I would watch him pray, watch him worship, watch him preach, watch him prophesy and tears would roll down my face. I craved that height of the spirit. I craved the precision and sharpness of his easy-access into the spirit realm. He trained our ears and our sensitivity to hear God. It was during those years I would lay before God totally oblivious of time as visions would begin to unfold. I would race home to have a Psalm 63:1-2 experience.

Psalm 63:1-2 O God, thou art my God; early will I seek thee: my soul thirsteth for thee, my flesh longeth for thee in a dry and thirsty land, where no water is; To see thy power and thy glory, so as I have seen thee in the sanctuary.

Single Mother Syndrome

Let's take a hard turn here. Notice the scripture above said, "Early will I seek **THEE!**" Watch this! Has anyone ever had a man bailout on you in a relationship before the baby was even born? You were planning on him being there to rub your belly, feel the baby kick, and help you waddle around through stores shopping for the baby items. Then due to whatever episode taking place, he decides he does not want to be a part of the baby's birth, or your life. Now you have to readjust to carry alone. Never thought you would be a single mother. Some are even crazy enough to ask for a divorce in the most critical time of your pregnancy. This living breathing seed is on the inside of you, waiting to be delivered, raised, and loved.

As much as I was grateful and dependent upon my spiritual father, one day he decided to jump up, close the church, and move back to his home state 13 hours away. For several years, I had to take what I became pregnant with in that ministry and learn to survive on my own, with my new baby. I couldn't call him when I went into a realm I did not understand anymore. I could not call him because my gift was crying out for its father. I had to come to a swift realization that though the release came through him, the deposit was released from God.

Therefore, we cannot become stuck on people, routines, organizations, denominations, and systems. We must seek God and God alone! People have the potential to fail, and oftentimes they will. It almost destroyed me because I did not believe anyone else could finish birthing me in the prophetic and in intercession but him. I was used to his dialect, his flow, his sound, his ability to pray that God would arrest us in His glory and disturb our sleep. By the time we would get home, no one could sleep. My seed was used to responding to his voice.

Yet, when he left I began to roam around searching for his sequel in other pastors. I became angry and disgruntle because they couldn't be him. I was disappointed that they could not pick up where he left off. Have you ever got introduced to a step-father after your father passed away, or after your parents divorced? I don't care how great the new dad was. He could buy you everything. He wasn't your biological father.

Let me emphasize this. Yes, it is vital to have a leader that is the mascot of prayer; one who leads and sets the pace for prayer in their congregation. However, leaders must embed a love for prayer in the sheep, without causing the sheep to be dependent upon them. Create an ambiance that produces a

God-culture. Let them see you do it, and they will be compelled to follow your lead. Brand them, smear them with the oil of God.

People often ask me what is the first thing I teach mentees, those seeking to understand their spiritual gift, and those who desire to be birthed into a deeper place with God. I tell them Prayer! Anyone that has ever been a part of E.K.G. (Empowering a Kingdom Generation) my first question is, *"How often do you pray? How often do you pray in your heavenly language* (tongues)?"

Nine times out of ten their answer is, "*Not often.*" Great! Easy answer. Easy solution. The first assignment is always to pray 30 minutes to an hour a day until God extends it. Pray in English, and then pray in tongues for as long as the Holy Ghost will allow (1 Corinthians 14:15). You can literally hear and feel the ascension and the dialect change taking place. Do not be afraid of this shift! There is more to come regarding this. Then I have prayer sessions with them to make sure they are becoming comfortable with the process and I pray with them.

Any leader that is beyond being involved in prayer and leading his/her congregation into the presence of God, derails the opportunity for power and the climate of glory to fill their sanctuary. As kingly as David was he was not beyond prayer, he was not beyond worship, and certainly, he was not beyond praise.

Leaders you are the trailblazers for breakthrough. Those who serve and follow you will mimic your posture. This is why it is vital for intercessors, particularly prophetic intercessors, to be in a prophetic house; one that believes in saturating the sanctuary with intercession. Being aware that dilating (stretching our faith) the womb of the atmosphere delivers God's intended results. No matter how far, or abruptly my spiritual father left us, he left a seed! He created a glory movement that has not died to this day. I learned to be a single mother in the spirit.

These are the kinds of monkey wrenches God will allow to make you. He will not allow you to become too dependent upon anyone else other than Him. It is designed to mature you. Disappointments, torment, hurts, offense, and unexpected trauma is all part of the process. It is vital to go through constant deliverance, pressing out the afterbirth of situations you face. Intercessors who have had to change ministries for whatever reason, please empty out and heal before serving in new locations! The infections and poisons from previous places are still resting in your womb as you try to pick up and become pregnant with a new assignment.

I know I hurt a lot of leaders after my experience with being dropped, because I kept comparing them to my spiritual father in order to get the process complete in me. I judged leaders harshly without understanding things had to go the way they did to break me, purify me, and push me forward. I left churches prematurely. I probably went to churches I should have never joined. I didn't know how to come down out of the clouds of my past and live on the grounds of my future. It was destroying the puzzle I thought was complete in my mind as to how things were supposed to go. When my spiritual father moved back to his hometown, it was the most difficult journey of my life. I was thrusted back into the world of normality; church as usual, religion and tradition. Everything I declared I would never be connected to I had to submit to. I traveled around. I visited various churches and most often drove more than an hour for Sunday worship just to have a tolerable experience.

There will be seasons the Lord allows LIFE to be your maker, not just His hand. Prophetic people are often irritated, thrown in left field, and even find themselves disintegrating when they cannot find the atmosphere that is conducive to the Ruah of God. Even those unexpected sharp bends, curves, shifts of life teaches us how to handle the warfare of the unexpected in prayer. Guess what? To this day I am still learning how. Believe it or not, they both work hand in hand. It is the discipline of the spirit. Nothing about birthing prayer (prophetic prayer) can be predictable.

Religious churches that are determined not to shift from denominational rules and man-made boundaries seem to scuff up the womb of intercessors from the kicks and refusal to yield to God. Yet, as a prophetic intercessor, you have been charged to *Wait and Incubate* until you are released by God. It is the hardest labor to ever experience in life. It is a challenge you will never forget, but a test you must pass. The resistance is most intense and potent when the intercessor does not know who they are, and what they are charged to do. Remember your battle is not with flesh and blood. It is the enemy's attempt to cause you to miscarry in your second trimester of development.

Revelations 12:17 And the dragon was wroth with the woman, and went to make war with the remnant of her seed, which keep the commandments of God, and have the testimony of Jesus Christ.

This is not a literal woman, or seed being chased by a dragon, but it is a diabolical system that will attempt to come against the Kingdom of God. There must be an awareness of where to target your prayers. Know the systems and powers in high places that will seek to silence and abort your mission from heaven. Prophetic Intercessors need to be a part of an apostolic, or fully functioning five-fold ministry, if possible. The works and transitions of prayer need the detailed teamwork of prophetic voices and apostolic strategies.

This is another area that warfare comes to create barriers

for the prophetic intercessor because they know God is requiring more of them, but the culture of carnality often stifles their growth within the Church at large. New apostolic and prophetic leaders are now arising and discovering those hidden in the trenches. They are coming to the rescue to create ways of escape from religious systems. However, as I mentioned, for some this will be their training ground. They will be assigned to places that contradict what they carry. Their confidence in God's deposit must stand firm even when they are required to bring down the taunting spirit of Goliath. Don't be intimidated! Be Confident!

What happens when Nathan is assigned to David (2 Samuel 12)? What happens when Samuel is assigned to Eli (1Samuel 3)? What happens when David is assigned to a baby killer named Saul (1Samuel 18) and the Lord still says, "Carry the assignment full-term in prayer?" "But God there is no life here." "Carry It!" "But God my leader hates me and the very thing I have been called to do." "Carry It!" "But God I don't fit in. I am louder than everyone else. No one comes to prayer but me. They look at me crazy when You say go and lay at the altar in the middle of service." "Carry It!" "But God they don't believe in the prophetic." "Carry It!" "But God they told me to stop all of this carrying on. They don't operate like this." "Carry It!" Do you get the point? Excuses never excuse disobedience.

The journey of being broken and made by the hand of God

can be as short, or as long, as you allow. Before understanding the depth of submission most intercessors and prophetic people reek of rejection. They often find themselves leaving churches, planting here, and uprooting there. They began cycles of going back to places they've once departed. Hoping to right their wrongs and get peace at least to depart correctly. They return and discover things are the same, or sometimes worse. Some continue the frog hop from church to church to church and never get healed. Layers and layers of cycles will follow if the individual does not recognize their own patterns and seek deliverance for themselves whether assistance is offered, or not.

Then you have old faithful. Those who choose to submit to houses and leaders the right way. They never leave for 40 to 50 years, but have nothing to show for their longevity. Some are disgruntle because they realize a lifetime has passed and they have not grown. Others can't even identify their calling after 60 years. God honors their faithfulness, but they have been deprived of growth, maturity, and development. The nation is full of the most powerful change agents, tucked away in corners in silence so that they will not offend or shake up what's always been. God is sending a shaking that will resurrect an exceeding Great Army, the hidden valley of dry bones, needed to function in the Body of Christ in this hour (Ezekiel 37).

We are missing the prophetic army of the Kingdom because our Ezekiel prophets and intercessors have gone silent. Some are silent because God is purging rebellion, hurt, mixed impartations, and lack of discipline out of them. Others are silent under the guise of submission. It takes leaders after God's own heart to know the difference and to properly position you. It takes patience, love, diligence, relationship, rebuke, restoration, and healing for this process to be successful.

The Nausea of Pregnancy

There were some sickening days in my process to delivery. During my journey as a prophet and intercessor it was often tough to figure out my posture without the assistance needed. It was tough to identify necessary seasons of silence, while being thrusted into pulpits to preach, sing, pray, and prophesy. Ordinations and licensures were shoved into my hands as a *quick fix* to my needing development and real fathering. I questioned myself, "Am I ready, or just needed?" It takes having been trained on the backside of the mountain like David to have the wisdom and maturity to reject Saul's mantle (1Samuel 17:38-39).

You must know when accepting a promotion could destroy you. You must know that fighting with another's weapons could cause you to self-destruct. When there is not a contiguous voice of instruction to develop you, it is a dangerous responsibility. Nevertheless, the Church taught us to trust our leaders and their decisions without questioning them. That takes careful prayer, discernment, and knowing the voice of God in this hour. What you carry is critical. At the end of the day, you are responsible for your seed.

I often accepted ascensions without proper instructions or direction, hoping to keep peace by way of obedience. What happens when you get in the position because you look the part, but you're broken? What happens when you can deliver the sound, but you're bitter? What happens when you are everything the church wants you to be until you tap the place that no longer sounds like them? What happens when a DNA test is taken in the spirit and they realize they are not the father of your seed?

It can create a war when spiritual sons and daughters are released without definition, communication, or identification. They are more than just a gift and a sound. Underneath all those amazing gifts lies a soul, a heart, and a desire to be loved. The value of the vessel must exceed the quality of the gift. The test to what kind of son or daughter you are is how willing you are to serve without a title. Leaders must have the desire to serve before the desire to take a microphone. They need to see if you will come to intercessory prayer without having to lead it, when it's empty. Diligence, purification, and consistency should be *proven prior to promotion.*

Know this. It is never a real intercessor's desire to hurt their leader nor a ministry. Yet it is a critical process to pastoring them. The troublesome attachment of the prophetic only intensifies the problem. Is there a manual that helps the leader to know that this many complications would come with the territory of pastoring the unique? The easy thing to do is to ignore them, or silence them. Some even cut the umbilical cords attached to these individuals. Most times that is a sigh of relief for the submitted vessel when so many years of labor has been pulled out of them.

The prophetic intercessor becomes comfortable in their recess from being in position. They go through self-induced hysterectomies. *"God remove my ability to birth,"* they say. *"Then I won't have to be responsible for what I am not allowed to produce."* Doesn't it seem easier to just move to the back of the sanctuary and pretend it never existed? Isn't it easier to not have to feel the kicks, the pulls, the burdens, the unctions, the yearning to see the church grow and shift more than the one who pays the mortgage? Isn't it easier to just fit in?

This is where the rubber meets the road for both the intercessor and the pastor. The challenge for the intercessor, who also needs continued training and growth supported by a strong atmosphere, is critical.

The following must be a part of the equation:
1) eradicating frustration
2) remaining humble and submissive to whomever God assigns you to
3) recognizing the enemy behind the division and target the root in prayer
4) remaining refreshed in the presence of the Lord

Then the final and most seemingly devastating one is, reversing the hysterectomy in the spirit! You must remain open to bring forth! You must trust God with your womb, your heart, and your life as an intercessor. Shutting down on God to prevent the pain with man will destroy your mobility. If you can relate to anything I just described, you have probably stated at some point, *"I am pulling out of this place of prayer. I'm shutting down. I will never be the intercessor for another ministry. I don't ever want to feel those burdens again."* Be careful that you don't Despise what the Doctor (God) Prescribed.

Another blazing identification is to determine who impregnated you. God recently gave me a sneak peek into the cure for spiritual miscarriages and abortions, and it is to become pregnant with an eternal seed, which is the Word of God.

Isaiah 55:11 - So shall my word be that goeth forth out of my mouth: it shall not return unto me void, but it shall accomplish that which I please, and it shall prosper in the thing whereto I sent it.

Psalm 119:89 - Your word, LORD, is Eternal; it stands firm in the heavens.

This may sound a little rough, but pop in your spiritual dentures and chew. Many of you that have declared seasons of miscarriage and abortion, it was never the seed of God because His seed does not die! When leaders, mentors, spiritual fathers/mothers finish dropping and aborting you it often leaves you feeling rejected, broken, wounded and most of all barren. I believe that many of the seemingly unfortunate miscarriages and successful abortions were impregnations that took place by the wrong people, in the wrong atmospheres, with the wrong deposits.

God has declared over His children that, *"If it does not resemble Me - it cannot be birthed. So, I caused your womb to be as the whale of Jonah and miscarry, and regurgitate what did not belong there. Just as I will spew out the lukewarm* (Revelations 3:16), *I will cause your womb to reject what is not of Me and My DNA,"* says the Lord. Though you've cried over the loss, it was replaced with that which shall remain.

You've got to be careful as there are demonic spiritual fathers and mothers as well. They are called witches and warlocks. You've got to protect that which is in your womb. You've got to be sensitive enough to get fed in the spirit by God so you are not starving to the point where you crave food from the enemy's table. Don't be so desperate to be carried and birthed out by someone. Prophets and prophetic people tend to be very clingy when someone comes into our midst that seems deep, or that resembles what we are familiar with without trying the spirit to see if it be of God (1 John 4:1). Let the Holy Spirit decide what you receive.

Prophetic Insert and Release

I decree and declare in this moment that the Holy Ghost unties your tubes in the spirit! Every assignment you have been charged to carry out you will not abort! You will not miscarry! It will not be breeched! You will not pass the assignment off to another and give it up for adoption! You will live and not die in the process of birthing the will and the heart of the Father! Every time you declared you will never put yourself in that predicament again you found yourself pregnant!

You found yourself carrying your leaders heart even when he/she thought you was Jezebel sent to destroy them! Your seed hears the sound of the Father calling it forth! Your seed is responding and yielding with obedience! I call forth your Midwives! I call forth Fathers, not just Instructors! I command the walls and the barriers to break between leaders and intercessors and prophetic voices around this nation!

Leaders are hurt, wounded, broken, betrayed, misunderstood, disrespected, dishonored, confused, without answers! The same traits rest in those who follow you! The Lord calls the whole house healed today! There cannot be reproduction without the intercourse and consummation of love and humility. Both gifts need each other. The congregation needs the parenting and the marriage of the prophet and the pastor, the pastor and the intercessors, and the merging of the church families.

We decree a mending of broken covenants across this nation. There are spiritual fathers and mothers who have gone years without speaking to your spiritual daughters and sons who are now somewhere on the other side of the world. They need to hear your voice. You need to hear theirs. Your church hasn't been the same without them. Not because you couldn't do it without them, but because God assigned them and both aborted the process, God is not pleased.

Traveling prophets and preachers, your ministry has not been the same since you disconnected from your covenant parents. Go back and correct it. Go back and restore relationship. It does not mean all of you will reconnect as members, but mend the threefold cord that was broken. The healing we need in our land must start from inside the household of faith and then spread abroad.

There is so much healing needed in so many areas of the Body for the ministry of intercession to be restored. I have erased, rewritten, revamped, reworded so much in this book so that it comes out the right way. I've tweaked it so that it is not offensive to leaders, but also not eradicating the hidden truths necessary to bring healing to many of you who need to get back on your posts. All you needed to know was that it is real, and you are not the only one.

I will close this chapter addressing some difficult things. Why? Because you did not need another How-To Intercede booklet. Many of you are more gifted than you know. It's been the delay of your process that has stunted your growth. I am putting my reputation and my life on the line to tell you I know and I understand but you cannot stop, and you cannot quit because of the warfare of being an intercessor. Yes, it is part of every trimester.

Many of you have found yourselves lost in the wilderness searching for your match in the spirit. You are looking for a church that is free. You long for a fervent five-fold prophetic/apostolic operation. You are craving a ministry strong in intercession, explosive praise and worship, and a house that trains and releases. You most definitely don't want to be deprived of dynamic preaching and teaching with the demonstration of miracles, signs, wonders, and deliverance. That's a large package, right?

Most prophetic intercessors thrive off of these. For some regions, it is far and few in between to find a church that is a perfect fit for you. So, what must happen in the process? You must be circumcised to fit the mold of your assigned local ministry. That means extract what you feel. You need to function where you are sent. The Bible says it like this, *"Lay aside every weight and the sin that so easily besets us, and let us run with patience the race that is set before us* (Hebrews 12:1).

Just as you want leaders to be patient with you, you must be patient with the developmental phase of the ministry. Make sure you are part of the building process. We must cut off the spirit of analyzing. If you are like me, if things just made sense you could do it with ease. Thus, many of you are even a part of prophetic and apostolic houses that has all the perfect verbiage. They take claim to being Prophetic, Apostolic, Kingdom and cutting edge with no manifestation.

There goes the frustration again, because your mind is saying, "If it were unbelievers, or even religious people, at least there would be a diagnosis. The perfect face and image is here, but we are lacking power and manifestation!" It hurts because of the level of expectation. It hurts because of the criticism of seemingly like DNA. Prophets are warring against Prophets. Apostles are warring against Apostles. Intercessors are warring against Intercessors.

Psalm 55:12-15 (KJV) For it was not an enemy that reproached me; then I could have borne it: neither was it he that hated me that did magnify himself against me; then I would have hid myself from him: But it was thou, a man mine equal, my guide, and mine acquaintance. We took sweet counsel together, and walked unto the house of God in company.

The frustration sits in our atmospheres like swamp water. We must heal from each other's criticisms. The inability to embrace each other's differences has caused a major destruction. What about the silent warrior? Many of you have felt disqualified as prayer warriors because you don't sound like the loud, seemingly, powerful voices who should be your co-laborers in prayer. Many have counted themselves out, nor do they feel worthy to pray. You despise the soft delicate sound that you produce. This may seem like a very small matter for a book such as this, but these are the small foxes that have destroyed the vines of our growth. Loose the comparisons. I say to you that you are a silent force in the earth. Healing must fill those wounds.

It is these small things that will cause a person to drop out of their posture and position as a gatekeeper. The Lord is saying, "Let it go, and revisit your worth in Me. I made you and I gave you your sound. Do not compare, nor contradict your effectiveness based on another's operation. Yes, you must come forth! There is power and greatness in you. Be healed and come forth!"

God is Healing the Womb of Leaders

There is almost too much to even un-package for this book alone. I know I should be giving step-by-step information and direction for prayer. However, we must deal with what really needs to be addressed in prayer; things that so often get ignored. Right now, I want to hone in on the tender areas for leaders that need prayer. They are not beyond restoration. There are good leaders, with pure hearts who feel like they are fighting losing battles. As a matter of fact, they need it more because they have to lead and be perfected while on display. How many prophetic intercessors pick up their hearts, their fears, their burdens and idiosyncrasies? How many can see past their smiles and loving on the people?

There is a multiplicity of leaders that were never trained, fathered, or equipped. Some were voted into position as pastor. It happens you know! It's like a newborn baby being left on your front doorstep with a note saying, *"PLEASE RAISE MY BABY!"*. It's like having the obligation of raising a deceased sibling's child. Many of you inherited your father's church and did not want to disappoint him in his passing. You didn't go through, what you felt like, was proper preparation to pastor. You inherited another man's burden. That's the funny part about DNA and family. You often inherit responsibilities before you inherit the birthright. There is a multiplicity of stories and reads about *The Process to the Birthright*: (Genesis 37:19-22; Genesis 49:1-4; Genesis 49:22-26; (2 Chronicles 11:18-23).

Now many of you are frustrated because God has sent people to you before you could get training on how to train or lead? You never knew much of this existed, or that you would have people of this caliber to pastor. It makes you feel inadequate, but you will never admit it. All you know to do is preach well. Now you're saying, "What is all the birthing, intercession, and warring about?" Pastor, God is sending you midwives, prophets, trainers, and intercessors to help catapult your ministry to the next place, but you've got to *break* the *brakes* off and trust Him. Some of you aren't as abrasive or controlling as others, but you are quiet and you skate around what you are realizing is needed in your church.

Pastors, many of your leaders aborted their process in making you. They never properly released you. You just had to step out and obey God and start the church because God wouldn't let you ignore it any longer. They spoke against you and told you that it was not your time. You left hurt and incomplete. Some of you are prophets and apostles that pastor prophetic people, but the cycles continue because no one properly fathered you? Now you inflict the same abuse upon your people. There must be a pause to allow God to be the Master Voice in our nation!

As I am typing this, we just received information today on November 8th, 2016, that Donald Trump is now the president of the United States of America. He has no prior political experience to support the power he is now possessing, but he has been given the office and responsibility to carry a nation who is depending on him. The power is in your hands to lead, but you must trust those who have been sent to help you to deliver. That place begins with intercession.

Let me speak to the Leaders who are intercessors and your congregation is rebellious, religious, and wants to vote you out (if it is that kind of ministry). They threaten to leave, or not sow seed, if you so much as change the paint on the walls. Do not let rebellious voices alter your decisions. Do not make them elders, ministers, prophets, intercessors, or leaders of any kind to have a hand in contaminating your vision. That is your baby! When a person comes in that is more interested in getting a microphone than they are in hearing your heart, stand clear of them! Guard your borders! Protect your sheep!

Even if it is too shameful for you to admit to your congregation that you simply don't know how to train, slip away and get training on your own. Better yet, humble yourself and lay at the altar with your congregation and ask the Father to impart His seed in the atmosphere. Give Him the liberty to build the house on the foundation of prayer and overtake your services with His glory. You will never fail! Be willing to admit when you are wrong. Be willing to cry in front of your congregation and be broken before the Lord.

Produce the seed you desire to see multiplied within your people. You cannot expand what you do not produce. The people will honor and respect your transparency. If they refuse to support prayer and submission before God first, they will never support you. Jesus was the first partaker of prayer but realized those following Him could not tarry with Him an hour (Matthew 26:40). Be the groundbreaker to prayer in your ministry. The seed will take root and produce much fruit.

Chapter Three
Shift Your Posture and Prepare to Push

"Discovering the Shifts, Moves, and Development of Your Seed"

From a different perspective, prophetic intercessors, midwives, those called to birth others into their purpose – don't be so quick to embrace everyone who cries out for your oil and assistance to birth them and assist them. Many of us are very sensitive and quick to birth people out and take them under our wings because we know what it feels like to be aborted.

Considering we know what it feels like for leaders not to take the time to train us, we move out of compassion. We try to embrace everybody with a tear in their eye and a hunger. The enemy uses that to play on your sympathy. The first thing you need to decipher is *hunger* from *hype*. Use discernment as Peter and John rebuked Simon in Acts 8:20-23 because he tried to buy the gifts of God for selfish and demonic purposes.

There are people who only want to be birthed out by you to obtain knowledge of your process for their purpose. Some never intend to pray on their own, fast, read the Word, or anything that requires effort on their end. It's just exciting to experience something new and electrifying. They don't intend to submit to anybody, with or without help. There's some male and female Delilah's that just want to know your secrets so they can lock you up and shut you down. They are sent by the enemy to keep you from being effective in tearing down the Kingdom of darkness. Prophetic intercession requires sensitivity, but most of all it requires the skill of the Holy Ghost and Wisdom.

You've got to know the difference between "desperation" and "demonation". There are some devils that will come in your midst and act like they are a part of you, act like they are there to help you pray and labor and accomplish the purpose of the Lord, when in fact they have come to stop your process (Ezra 4:1-5). I even feel a prophetic shift as I am typing and revamping this prophetic chapter on intercession.

I pause now to speak to the womb of your spirit. I speak to the shell that protects your seed that it will be laced with the repellant of the blood of Jesus against every demonic force that will come to frustrate and eliminate your purpose in the earth. Every demonic force of wickedness in high places, according to Ephesians 6:12, that will attempt to eradicate prayers and intercession that is stored up in your belly to bring change to your regions, to your church, to your leaders, to your nation. I speak paralysis to the hands that reach out from demonic realms to choke the life out of your seed. I speak paralysis to the movement of the enemy's plan.

We shred the blueprint of the enemy now in the name of the Lord Jesus and we speak an eternal abortion and barrenness to the womb of the enemy, to the womb of Hell in Jesus name. We declare no more reproduction from the enemy's camp. We declare not another day of abortions and miscarriages from the citizens of the Kingdom of our Lord. We declare that you will carry full term. We declare a healthy ministry. We declare victory over the Lord's people in Jesus' mighty and wondrous name.

How do you know when you are pregnant with a God seed and not just anxious to do something? He always backs it up with His Word. For the longest while, people would bombard me with questions about defining a prophetic midwife. Initially I did not know how to fully explain, or even give examples of it biblically myself. I just knew I was called to it. You have the midwife in Genesis the 38th chapter that identified the breaking forth of Perez. Had she not tied the scarlet string around the baby's wrist they would not have known that there was a breaking forth of the unexpected.

In Exodus 1:17 it tells us that the midwives feared God and did not do what the king of Egypt told them to do; they let the boys live. If there were more midwives in the Body of Christ hearing the instruction of the Lord and preserving the life of the Church, when the enemy sets out to destroy the reproductive system, there would be more fruitfulness and multiplication of gifts. However, until Zion bears down and travails in prayer and supplication we will continue to see a major decline in the Five-Fold Ministry.

Someone will probably say, "Well I thought you just said there are no miscarriages in God?" There are no miscarriages if we remain pregnant with His purpose, His will, and His Word. So often we fall away from God's system and still expect God's benefits while employed by the World. The Body has become a harlot, going a whoring after other gods that have occupied the space of God.

Judges 2:17KJV - "And yet they would not hearken unto their judges, but they went a whoring after other gods, and bowed themselves unto them: they turned quickly out of the way which their fathers walked in, obeying the commandments of the LORD; but they did not so."

Let me reference to *Discovering the Shifts, Moves, and Development of Your Seed* again for one moment. After several years of traveling in the realm of the spirit (moving from one destination in prayer to another) I came to understand the purpose and significance of how prophetic intercession works. Let me pause and define what most prophets, or intercessors, call "traveling in the spirit." I've been using that term through the whole book without fully defining it.

Take the word *travel* from a natural standpoint. Per

Merriam-Webster dictionary, travel means to move in a given direction, path, or through a given distance; to move from one place to another; to journey through, or over. I especially like the last one "to journey through or over." This is what happens in the spirit when our spirit man launches out into the deep. We take a journey into places we cannot go physically.

For example, one night I was in prayer and as usual my tongues began to shift into an African dialect. I began to see villages, huts, soldiers, and even others of foreign descent. I saw what looked like a war in Africa. I saw people being forced underground by armed soldiers. The spirit of the Lord told me to go and turn the television on. I rebuked the enemy. I told the devil he would not pull me off my face as the Lord was now tapping me into a place I had never been, but again the spirit of the Lord said to turn the television on.

I continued to pray in tongues, but I rose out of my bed where I had been stretched out interceding, and I walked into the living room and turned on the television. My mouth immediately dropped. There was a documentary on the television about a war in Darfur, Africa. I had no idea what was going on, or why the same visions I had just seen in prayer were on my television screen. It motivated me even more to pray through for those people. I knew there had been a connection made in the spirit.

There was no way for me to know what was taking place in

Africa and I live in Birmingham, Alabama other than to travel in the spirit and allow the Holy Spirit to pray through me what was needed to connect with the intercessors in that country. Intercessors, you are pretty much catapulted from a physical location to a spiritual destination. Knowing the type of intercessor you are called to be is half the battle.

There are crisis intercessors, intercessors of healing, marketplace intercessors, regional intercessors, and so much more. It is common for intercessors to have a desire to pray all the time, but there is an extremely intense pull, or summonsing, when there is a specific need for your kind of intercession. Most times, I am an intercessor called to birth people out, or push them forward in delivering their spiritual gifts; whatever God has called them to do. Often when I am in a service and someone is at the altar wrestling with the call to intercession or the prophetic and it seems to be locked up in them, the host, or pastor will call me to lay hands on them to birth out and pray for their release because they know that I will pick up the burden and compassion to pray them through.

Prophetic Transitions of Prayer

What does it mean to *pray through*? It means to pray until the burden of the Lord lifts. It means stand your ground and don't come off of your post until the Father releases you. When the weight of prayer hits us in our bellies to cry out to God, we begin to travail, or cry with agony. Let the sound of travail be heard. Carry the sound of the ram's horn in your belly. God is crying with you, for you, and through you. The intensity, severity, or weight of the situation at hand fuels the strength of our prayers. When David fasted, and went in for the child he bore with Uriah and the Lord struck the child with sickness, David would not eat and he cried out before God all night because of the severity of the situation. Once he learned the child had died he rose, washed his face, and ate (2 Samuel 12).

In the natural, his burden lifted because the child died, but in the spirit realm we pray until the Lord says it's enough or you feel the conclusion of the matter in prayer. How do you know? The drive and the weight lightens. Sometimes you can become repetitive and there is no weight to your words. The Holy Ghost has taken a seat from praying through you at that point so it is to be released and trusted in faith that the Lord has heard your prayer.

I know this is not a book on the prophetic, but since I am a prophet, clearly you have seen the pattern by now in my verbiage. I must address all perspectives because all prophets are intercessors, but not all intercessors are prophets. Let me take a moment to deal with the prophets who are also intercessors.

People often wonder why prophets seem so unstable, and fickle, and it's so hard for them to be satisfied. I am not making excuses for instability, or failure to submit, but a true prophet who is submitted to God and His will just want to find food for his/her acquired taste. The prophetic, and even intercession, is an acquired taste. If you are not called to either you will probably hate their very flavor, flow, vernacular, and thought patterns.

An apostle once told me, "Prophets can't be loyal." What he was saying was they can't be locked into the confines of men's expectations for them. They are committed to God first, last and any transitional period between. They may have to make you mad in order to please God. Here is another good place to plug in one of my Facebook blogs.

Thursday, January 22, 2015

Listen Prophets you're not CRAZY!!!! (beats on the mic) I repeat...You're Not Crazy!!!! Feeling a little schizo??? One minute you're preaching, prophesying, laying hands, feeling the weight of God...then suddenly get an impact of Woe is me??? You're not crazy! You're a Prophet! Remember Elijah's crazy self? You mean to tell me you can call down fire and you got the nerve to be running from Jezebel? Sir...do you not know who you are??? LOL!!! Yeah well most don't. We operate by uncontrollable God unctions.

Therefore, as you are sitting under the juniper trees of life and the ministering angels of the Lord come to feed you (when His presence comes to feed you) you must eat hardily for the journey ahead. When those portals of worship open during service and people wonder why you won't settle down, they think you are just being deep. Say to them "Pardon me precious, please don't bother me while I'm eating. I need this substance for what I am called to do. It might not take a lot of food for what you do, but I need my Wheaties for the devils I got to fight! I need protein for the witches and warlocks that's on my trail."

When those moments of weighty glory come and it seems like you can't shake it...Don't!!! You may be the only person at the altar! You may be the only one left standing with your hands lifted!!! The angel told Elijah Eat Some More for the journey ahead of you is great!!! I say to you Eat Some More!!!! You're going to need substance, rest, and power for this next place. Again, I say You're Not Crazy...You're A Prophet!

We are beings called unto the deep. You have to be in order to be the ones with whom God chooses to share his secrets. No one wants to talk to someone shallow that does not speak their language AND take pleasure in it. It doesn't make your value any less because you're not a prophet. Prophets are just who God chooses for particular conversations.

Have you ever spoken to someone that you were close with and loved but just thought, "No I can't tell them this...?" As much as I love talking to them, they wouldn't understand?" What would a scientist look like talking to a football coach about his passion and his discoveries? It's two different worlds.

Choose your bonding place wisely, or yes people will think you are off your rocker. Have you ever had to keep a secret, but the secret contained information that could seriously affect those around you? Yet the person tells you not to release the information? This is the life of prophets, and even more so intercessors, because rarely are intercessors even allowed to speak what they hear and see. It must be birthed in prayer!

Amos 3:7 (KJV) Surely the Lord God will do nothing, unless He revealeth His secret unto His servants the prophets.

Driving the Vehicle of Prayer
through Realms and Dimensions

The spirit of the Lord will sometimes launch you into intercession that gives access to realms, dimensions, portals and experiences that are not so pleasant, but it's all for a purpose. As I found myself shifting, growing, prayer languages developing, I also discovered the unexpected manifestations of second dimensional warfare. I don't want to get into too much detail about dimensions and realms because it will shift the format of the book's focus and would require a greater depth of understanding and interpretation. However, if you have operated at any point and time in intercession, or more so, prophetic intercession, you are aware of at least the basics of first, second, and third dimensions.

The first dimension is, from a geographical standpoint, a point, or a line. It can only be measured in length, but not depth. Not to say prayer is based on how long you pray, but as mentioned in the first trimester regarding general prayer, most general intercessors pray for a long time, for long hours, every day, almost all day. Obviously, you are on the first floor of the spirit, earth. We operate by way of our five senses: seeing, hearing, tasting, touching, and smelling. God has given us the ability to rule and have dominion and authority over the earth. The following scriptures give reference to this fact.

Genesis 1:26 Then God said, "Let Us make man in Our image, according to Our likeness; let them have dominion over the fish of the sea, over the birds of the air, and over the cattle, over all the earth and over every creeping thing that creeps on the earth."

Genesis 1:28 Then God blessed them, and God said to them, "Be fruitful and multiply; fill the earth and subdue it; have dominion over the fish of the sea, over the birds of the air, and over every living thing that moves on the earth."

As you ascend into the second dimension, you shift into the place where your soul, mind, and emotions are often strongly affected. In the second dimension one expands to operate not only in length, as the first dimension, but in length and in width.

Ephesians 3:16-18(KJV) That he would grant you, according to the riches of his glory, to be strengthened with might by his Spirit in the inner man; That Christ may dwell in your hearts by faith; that ye, being rooted and grounded in love. May be able to comprehend with all saints what is the breadth, and length, and depth, and height;

The way things are viewed from a prophetic intercessor are more broad. It's not just how long we pray, but we pray the secrets of God's heart towards the root of the situation. Satan was thrown out of the third heaven to earth where we dwell, but he rules from the second heaven (Revelations 12:7-12). This is the place where warfare can appear with any opposing spirit that attempts to hinder the work of Christ in the earth. There is warfare from witches, warlocks, demons, principalities such as Leviathan, and underworld manifestations in the second dimension.

2 Corinthians 10:4-5 (KJV)
For the weapons of our warfare are not carnal, but mighty through God to the pulling down of strong holds; Casting down imaginations, and every high thing that exalteth itself against

the knowledge of God, and bringing into captivity every thought to the obedience of Christ;

Daniel 10:12-13 (KJV)
Then said he unto me, Fear not, Daniel: for from the first day that thou didst set thine heart to understand, and to chasten thyself before thy God, thy words were heard, and I am come for thy words. But the prince of the kingdom of Persia withstood me one and twenty days: but, lo, Michael, one of the chief princes, came to help me; and I remained there with the kings of Persia.

Let me share another personal experience I had years ago as I was breaking into prophetic intercession. I was already in a consistent flow of just wanting to be closer to God. I would come straight home from work, lay on my face for hours, and pray in tongues. Well my spiritual father asked us to cover him during his trip back to Chicago for a ministry assignment. He was always on the road, but this time it felt different. I prayed, but what took place that night, I was nowhere near prepared to face.

As my tongues shifted into a sound I had never experienced before, I began to see a vision of a witch. The very image of it would raise the hair on your body. Of course, at this point I thought I had slipped off into something that was not God. I tried pulling out, but that is virtually impossible after having ascended into this place in prayer for hours. It was going to take time to get out of that zone.

I tried opening my eyes thinking the tongues would subside and the image would go away, but it did not. She kept reaching and clawing at me, but every time the tongues would come forth, she would jump back. It was as if the language coming out of my mouth was acid on her skin. I finally shook myself and held my mouth to stop anything else from coming out.

I spoke to my spiritual father the next day and told him what happened. He reprimanded me and said, "You left me uncovered, Lissa." I had no idea what he meant. He said, "You stated you were praying for me, right? Well this is what happened..." He commenced to tell me that the Lord began to show him someone that was against the pastor's ministry he was preaching for. He began to call out certain activities that were taking place and the leader agreed.

He narrowed down the description to a woman in the ministry who had been there for years. Come to find out she had been working witchcraft in the ministry the reason it was not growing. She refused deliverance that night and left. Later on, she astro-projected her image into his room and asked why he was in their region. He said he was on assignment and commanded the spirit to go. It did, but not without leaving an attack behind. He woke up the next morning broke out in hives and had a fever. He could not board the plane until his temperature came down. He said to me you never pull out of a place of intercession especially when the Lord is pulling you heavily into it.

There is something He wants you to pray through, or cover, and you leave doors open and matters undealt with when you pull out of prayer before the burden lifts. That was my first, second dimension experience at the age of twenty-one. I was beginning to learn the severity of life and death battles and how they can be shifted, halted, or terminated by the mere release of divine intercession.

There was another experience I had while at my job. The Lord began to drop someone in my spirit that I had not seen in years. They had been sick, but I did not know of any change in their status. They were also sick with an illness many people recover from and continue in life. Well after maybe a few years of not seeing or hearing from them, they dropped on me like a ton of bricks. Initially I thought about checking on them when I got off work, but the Holy Ghost dropped them on me again and gave me a nudge to move right then.

I got up from my desk and walked into a nearby conference room to make a few calls to see if anyone had heard from him. Each call I made my spirit became more frantic. I made enough calls for people to reach out and start checking on the person, but before I could leave out of the conference room, I was in tears. I literally had to log out and go home. I called my supervisor from my car. That is how intense the weight became.

As I was driving home, it was drizzling and very gloomy outside. The car lights approaching looked like a funeral procession. I kept trying to pray for the individual's life, but the spirit of the Lord said, "Do not pray for his life, pray for his soul." I fought it until the Lord would not let me pray in English. I was forced to pray in tongues. He was determined to get His will out of me, though I wanted to shift His plan.

When I arrived home the Lord told me to take his picture out and lay on it. I followed Holy Spirit's directions. As I laid on his picture, I cried so hard and prayed so intensely. An image of his face appeared before me. I could see his head laying back on a pillow and his breathing was shallow. I could see him attempting to pray and speak in tongues with the last breath that was in his body. Then I took a hard breath and it was over.

I got up and dried my face, but when I spoke to a few people I asked them to continue praying for him because I did not feel like he was going to make it through the night or for a few days.

The next morning, I woke up and my best friend called and asked if I had gotten the news. He was gone. I think that experience shook me like nothing has ever shaken me before. I went through the normal emotions of guilt, inadequacy, failure, and a host of other feelings because I wanted him to live. The first thing I did was searched myself to see if it was anything I could have done differently.

The challenge for any intercessor is hearing God and following through with His plan. Thus, faith is a mandatory ingredient of operation in our lives. We must know and be sure that our confidence is in Christ and that we have followed through with what He has assigned to us in prayer.

Here's another very short example of mandatory obedience. I was around the age of 22. I had traveled for years with community choirs, did back up for various recording artists performing special events, and more. I was very open, very sensitive, and visions came a dime a dozen. I was in the salon getting my hair done when the power of God fell on me under the dryer. I told you God does not care where He comes in. Thank goodness my best friend was my hairstylist. I start crying and seeing visions of various nationalities swirling around in a bubble. I saw Africans, Asians, and probably even nationalities I couldn't quite describe.

Well the image of Asians swelled up larger than the others and appeared before me. At this point of my life as an intercessor I had come to know how critical it was to pray fervently when visions like this appeared. I didn't know if destruction was coming or what was about to happen to these people. I just knew I needed to pray in the Holy Ghost.

Shortly after the Lord kept giving me words to get my passport. I was thinking how low my bank account was. I didn't have enough money to get across town. I ignored the word over and over again. I started to have weird dreams about hotels in another country where water was flowing through a glass as I walked in the hotel. Still no clue where. Not long after I was asked to take a trip suddenly to Japan to sing with a mission's group/choir.

It was a full-expense paid trip for an entire week. I was working a temporary job. The director of this choir paid me to sing, paid me for time off, paid for flight, hotel, and food. The only problem was we had to travel to New Orleans to get a passport as soon as possible because I didn't obey God and get the passport when He told me to. I even got to the hotel in Nagoya and there was the stream of water built into the crosswalk just as I had dreamed.

There are countless stories I could share like these. However, I am not telling them to validate or prove my effectiveness. I want to help build your faith and confidence in the things God entrusts to you. The purpose of these testimonies is so that you can understand you *Can Not Take Things Lightly*. Most of you either already have, or you will have the testimony that people think you are crazy.

You will often second-guess your calling, or you may even think you are losing your mind because of the continual jolts of

God, when He yanks you from one place to the next it is often mind-boggling until you become acclimated to the unpredictable shifts of the Lord.

Soon it even becomes a part of your makeup as an intercessor. If you are a prophetic individual, or have an apostolic anointing on your life, more than likely this has been your "make up" since you were born. The power and effectiveness of the gift flows much more fluently when we embrace and agree with the calling of God on our lives.

Do you know the enemy uses doubt to silence us? God gave me a word that I shared a short while ago to prophets via Facebook. It happens to be one of my favorite ways to blog and reach people, and this applies to all prophetic people and His Kingdom mouthpieces in the earth.

January 6, 2015

PROPHETS!!! – I saw a vision of many of you with cobwebs and debris in your mouth...down your throats. And I see the breath of God blowing your mouth out. Blowing out the dust in your throats from being closed. That's how long some of you have been silent. That's how long it's been since some of you have spoken the word of the Lord! It's like an old empty house where there has been no movement, no sound, no activity.

It has drawn things that sit and make their domain in places where there is darkness, where it is dank, where it is still and lifeless, but the Father is sending the light of His prophet to shine a light down your throat and rescue your breath. For the breath of the Lord is your eternal life. The Spirit of Ezekiel comes to rescue you out of the dungeon of stagnancy and death. Your sound must live! I command the alarm to return to your voice. Blow Trumpet Blow!!!

Open the cracks and crevices of your spirit! For I will come and make habitation again in your voice. I speak to the cemetery of your soul!!! I call you out of the grave and the cave that you have made your hiding place. Like a traveler who once shipwrecked and made a new life on a deserted island. After a while, you gave up on being found!!!

You gave up on finding an apostle, a prophet, or a spiritual father that you could trust to awaken the unique gift on the inside of you! You gave up on finding one who could even locate your larynx in the spirit!!! You gave up on finding a pure leader that would not hurt you, abuse you, prostitute you, mishandle you, or abort you! You learned how to live in the wilderness.

You learned to make that deserted island your home! But the Father says I am coming to rescue my prophets!!!! You shall not die but live to declare the Works and the Word of the Lord!!!! Wave your white flag!!! Surrender!!!! You have been found!!! And you shall come forth says the Spirit of the Living God!

You've got to know the power and the ability of what you are pregnant with. Are you skilled, by the hand of the Lord, in maneuvering through the realm of the spirit via prophetic intercession? If so, then you must begin to understand your authority and your ability to make things happen because the Word says so!

The Bible says in Revelations 2:7, "*He that hath an ear, let him hear what the Spirit is saying unto the Church.*" Though you may, or may not be a prophet walking in the office, you can prophesy even through prayer. We make declarations to decree things to be so.

2 Chronicles 20:20 (KJV) And they rose early in the morning, and went forth into the wilderness of Tekoa: and as they went forth, Jehoshaphat stood and said, Hear me, O Judah, and ye inhabitants of Jerusalem; Believe in the LORD your God, so shall ye be established; believe his prophets, so shall ye prosper.

There is a place of promotion in the realm of the spirit. Much of it develops in you as you discover and become confident in your sphere of influence. As an executor of the purpose of the Lord, the Earth begins to respond to your sound, your existence, and mandate! Once you understand where your authority lies, that is where you are graced to ascend in intercession. It is the place where you operate geographically according to the parameters of grace given by

God. In other words, *Know your Trimester*! Never attempt to carry, birth, or deliver on a level you have not been stretched. Labor in prayer produces Seed in the Kingdom!

You learn to drive into those places with everything in you. I know that I am graced to flow in the spirit to parts of Africa, Asia, and other foreign territories. If you are not graced to go there, never try to compete in comparison to others' assignments. Maturity, strategies and prophetic blueprints are birthed out during these prayer journeys. Thus, transitioning many into the role of decreeing, declaring, and establishing in the functions and role of Apostolic Intercession.

Chapter Four
The Third Trimester: Manifestation
Apostolic Intercession

Ready! Aim! Fire!

"Bring Forth"

Before we drive further into the extremities of Apostolic intercession, let me set a mile marker here. As mentioned before, there are various timeframes given as to how far is too far to abort during pregnancy. I want to say to you by this trimester, it is too late to turn back. At this junction, you are a general of prayer and prophetic intercession. By now, you have gone through the ringer. Just as any woman in her third trimester, you are so swollen you look like a pig, or so you think. You cannot do anything NORMAL! The only thing that even penetrates your brain is, *when can I get this baby* (assignment, ministry, gift, calling, etc...) *out of me?*

The baby is shifting, the body is shifting, and things are being set in the proper order for your baby to come forth. In the spirit, you are getting ready to deliver what you have labored with, studied, and incubated to full development. Let's touch on the icing of this type of intercession. The Apostolic sets order, builds strategies, and governs the functions of the

Kingdom. From this posture of intercession one may experience much stronger warfare, but your resilience to the enemy's attacks have also been fortified.

Though this place is still uncomfortable, it is tolerable for the purpose of manifestation. When you understand that the labor is worth the delivery, it helps motivate you through the pain. It fuels the intensity of your PUSH! Intercession on this level is more precise, released with even more specificity and authority, and the triggers of prayer are pulled with perfect precision. Ready! Aim! Fire!

Welcome to the third dimension, the place where He reigns and rules. It is a place where the authority of Christ in you births God's thoughts, mind, and actions through you to walk out His manifested purpose in the earth.

A few years ago, the Lord assigned me to a job position that shifted me from a prophetic place to an apostolic place. I never lost the operation of the prophetic, but my sphere of operation stretched into a broader territory in the spirit. One of my bosses was a vice president as well as a pastor. There was an immediate bond and connection when we met. It was the most surreal experience.

Given my strong Pentecostal upbringing, had I met him five years before, some of his words would have had me speaking in tongues and dancing all around his office. Thank God for something called process, which prepares us for manifested maturity.

This man sat across from me one day and said, "I'm pregnant with something. It's like I feel literal movement in my belly and I know God is calling me to bring forth ministry and the vision of my church in a whole new way." I looked at him expecting him to reveal that he heard I was a midwife or something. Until recently my name was *"Melissa 'Prophetic Midwife' Sanders"* on Facebook. He just looked at me. I pulled out my phone and showed him my name.

He teared up and looked at me in awe. He said, "You've got to be kidding me. God sent me a Midwife for an administrative assistant?" I guess I should not have been surprised after all of the pastors and great people God has allowed me to assist in birthing their vision, but He never ceases to amaze me. The rest is history.

The revelations the Lord gave me to help him orchestrate and strategize his vision and ministry was ridiculously phenomenal. The Lord showed me his posture, things he needed to do to shift his life, things he needed to do to shift his ministry, and even his family. The way that God would speak to me with divine counsel left me speechless. He allowed me to deliver the instructions as if I were an expert. That was not the case.

The correlation between the marketplace and Apostolic-Prophetic jargon absolutely blew my mind. Since we have been connected, he has strongly embraced his call to the prophetic. Many on his ministry team have been filled with the Holy Ghost, speaking in tongues. His ministry is growing and our assignments are becoming clearer every day. Our dialogue began to sharpen and even birth something in me that helped me to take notice to the shift that had taken place.

As an apostolic intercessor, I am assigned to shift this region in prayer with him. I am assigned to pray over governmental and judicial decisions as he is given favor with mayors and council members in his area. He has been given access and favor into doors where decisions are made for our city. I sit at his feet to deliver the heart of the Father and deliberate over various principles, ideologies, values, and standards to produce change and effectiveness around the region.

From his wisdom and both corporate and pastoral expertise, he could help me balance out emotions and overwhelming challenges that I faced as well. The conversations were refreshing and empowering. It was like having a prophetic roundtable in the marketplace. This place is called *mastering your mountain* (7 Mountains discussed earlier).

Apostolic Intercessors sit in favored and trustworthy positions as voices of counsel. God trusts you in the hands and in the presence of power and greatness. If you have pumped brakes, allowed the enemy to shut you up, and failed to press through as the Holy Ghost teaches you how to maneuver through each level of prayer, you will not be prepared for the weightier assignments.

Again, remember the posture of Nathan and Nehemiah? What if you are assigned to Kings? You must be able to tap in to taste-test the atmosphere (Nehemiah 1:11), and give directions, interpret mysteries, and give answers when the Kings call for them (Daniel 2:17). You must be like David and be sharpened by private experiences before being released to fight in the public battle.

David didn't just come out of nowhere and defeat Goliath. He had a lifetime of practice. You may be on the backside of the mountain now and may not understand why you are always shifted and carried off into other countries during prayer, but ride the waves of prayer. Ride those winds of power as long as they blow. Pour the oil until you run out of vessels. Train and release to those who will listen!

2Kings 4:3-5 (KJV) 3 Elisha said, "Go around and ask all your neighbors for empty jars. Don't ask for just a few. 4 Then go inside and shut the door behind you and your sons. Pour oil into all the jars, and as each is filled, put it to one side." 5 She left him and shut the door behind her and her sons. They brought the jars to her and she kept pouring. 6When all the jars were full, she said to her son, "Bring me another one. "But he replied, "There is not a jar left." Then the oil stopped flowing.

I must inject this testimony for your encouragement. Of course, I mentioned early on that the Lord has validated several times my intercession and call to Africa. However, nothing compares to the day I stood before nations because of those sacrifices. I went to support Apostle John Eckardt in Atlanta, Georgia, as it was rare that he ministers so close to my state. He had become a very influential apostolic voice in my life when I could not get help or proper training from others. After he finished ministering, he called me up to flow with him in prophetic worship.

That moment was so surreal because I was standing in the midst of an *African* fellowship with a representation of over 20 nations, many watching online. After service, the pastor of the local church, Pastor Chuzzy, asked me to come back and minister in song that night. While I was ministering, he called me forth to speak to the people on the prophetic.

I spoke about the many years I was counted out, called weird, and rejected because I carried nations like Africa in prayer and did not understand why. He stopped me mid-sentence and asked everyone from Africa to stand and to tell me what part of Africa they were from. Nigeria, Ghana, Kenya, and places I cannot even remember were announced.

Pastor Chuzzy looked me in the eyes and spoke of the warfare they had experienced in transition to America. He said, *"Your tears and your prayers has freed a nation. This is who your intercession was for."* Not many days after I received a call to go to Nakuru and Kisumu, Africa. With the counsel of some apostolic voices of counsel I decided against it for the moment. However, please understand the weight of your suffering and uniqueness.

It is not about you, but birthing whom you are called to. There were governmental decrees spoken and released to snatch the victory of a nation in the spirit as apostolic intercession took place that I did not always understand. Though when the authority of God came upon me I knew my jurisdiction in the spirit had shifted.

Apostolic Intercessors walk in your knowing power. The mind of God will rest on you during these shifts and transitions. You must let this mind be in you which was also in Christ Jesus to perform the greater works of Christ (Philippians 2:5; John 14:12).

Governing Prayer with the Weapon of Knowledge

Apostolic Intercessors be aware and knowledgeable of the kinds of chief spirits that will work against you, and even your ministry or leader. The Spirit of Leviathan – Job 41st chapter (Pride), The Spirit of the Python (Lifelessness), and The Spirit of Religion (Stagnancy) are most common in five-fold ministries. Knowing how to strategize with other intercessors and prophets without causing harm to the leader or ministry name takes much labor, prayer, wisdom, and brokenness.

Most intercessors must be extremely quiet and off radar during flare up seasons. Seasons when there may be lots of chaos, drama, confusion, tension, disagreements, betrayal, scandal, and exposure is taking place. Many intercessors encounter physical sickness, stress, and emotional trauma because of their persistence and territories that are crossed in prayer.

It is most common to hear about abortions in the first trimester. The enemy tries to startle the intercessor from the onset so that they will never believe they can accomplish what they need through prayer and quit. He uses spirits of isolation, manipulation, spiritual deprivation, and demonic interrogation to force us to lose our momentum.

In the second trimester when the wind of God begins pushing you, your seed is growing, and results are being produced he attempts to cause miscarriage. The second trimester often encounters the warfare of the second heaven, where Satan is the ruler of the power of the air (Ephesians 2:2; 6:12). It is the time when the adversary fights most. Knowing what kind of intercessor you are, the areas you target most, and the common adversary for your territory of prayer can prepare you for what is to come.

For example, if you are called to be an intercessor that targets healing, you will have to eat right, get rest and do the practical things to protect your body from natural attacks.

Then you must cover your body, mind, and spirit with the Word of God. Counterattacking anything that will attempt to hinder you as a healing agent in the spirit.

In the third trimester breeched births (The Spirit of Error), Stillborn (The Spirit of Death), Umbilical cord-wrap (The Python Spirit), Premature Birthing (Missing God's Timing), and more seeks to attack. Just because you have almost completed the process to delivering the manifestation of the promise over your life the enemy is angrier than ever. In this time of maturity, growth, and development for yourself and those connected to you, it is critical to follow strategic plans and paths to detour traps and barricades to delay your process.

How does this relate to apostolic intercession? Once you step over into this broad territory, the logistics of prayer changes. It is no longer an individual, a demon, or a location that becomes your warfare. It is regional, global, and universal prayers that disarm systems, ranks, and powers. Typically, apostolic intercessors form teams and alliances to assist in targeting the focal areas due to the severity. It is not an individual assignment.

The journey is often tedious, complicated, and requires advanced strategies and insight. This is not the intercessor who takes the microphone to pray at church. This may be the intercessor that the Lord has taken off of their 8-5 job, give them an evangelistic prayer ministry that finances their living, and they may be charged to go to Washington, D.C. to pray at the White House.

Apostolic Intercessors such as Dutch Sheets and Chuck Pierce are often sought after by government officials and those in high offices for godly counsel, prayer, and the next set of instructions. Training and preparation is necessary early on, as you may not know the height and depth the Lord will take you to invoke change.

"Threatening A Breeched Birth"

I will not go through defining or addressing each of the birth complications listed above, but I particularly want to deal with *breeched births* due to the spirit of error that has entered the earth in this dispensation. What is a breeched birth?

"By around 8 months, there's not much room in the uterus. Most babies maximize their cramped quarters by settling in head down, in what's known as a cephalic presentation. However, if your baby is breeched, it means he's poised to come out buttocks or feet first."[3]

There is a major posture change that must take place in the Body of Christ in general, but there is a posture change for the apostolic intercessor that cannot be an option if you are going to be effective. Why? There must be a concrete alignment from the lips of any apostolic voice in the earth because of the critical sensitivity to what is entrusted in their hands.

Remember you now speak *as* God. Your words, your prayers, your counsel is being beckoned as a vocal GPS to the people of God. Your tenure, your track record, and your history with God demands a different kind of responsibility.

Therefore, in this trimester the seed is turning to make an exit. If nothing else depends on a healthy delivery, the posture in which the baby is coming out is crucial! There must be godly detail to:

- How your prayers are released
- When/Where your prayers are released
- Who your prayers are released for/against
- What your prayers target when released

Where: Be aware that your geographical location can make a world of difference in your influence and level of release. There are economic, educational, and governmental shifts that take place in various regions that can catapult or stagnate your movement. You do not want to be in error, pressing strong, but moving wrong.

As we get closer to apocalyptic times it does not mean it is time to panic, but it is most definitely a time to listen and prepare. After several years of governing your life to operate solely on the voice of the Lord it brings a sobering, confidence, and consistency in your patterns of operation in prayer and movement.

God has been known to speak to people to shift their entire

lives because they dared to listen and obey. He has been known to save entire families because they got out of harm's way. Lot and his wife were prime examples in Genesis the 19th chapter. God speaks to those in this manner that is willing to listen. He may speak to you to move to another part of the country because of destruction that is coming, famine, or even war.

Moving to that new state can open doors for wealth increase, divine connections, and restoration to position you for new assignments. Be where God is aligning you to speak. Favor comes with obedience and will open doors in various regions with people in high places to launch you forward. Favor will call you out to amplify your voice and give platforms you may not have in your hometown so that a greater multitude can be reached to hear the word of the Lord.

When revival is being sent to a particular region, the Father will begin to send apostolic prophetic teams, build apostolic hubs and layer the area with like voices to penetrate what needs to be broken with prayer and intercession. It is vital that apostolic intercessors Unify to Amplify! I believe that can even be applied to any level of intercession. Get with people who can help fuel what is on the inside of you so that there is a continual charge and echo of what the Father is speaking.

During some very rough patches in my process as an intercessor and prophet my only source of life was tapping into the presence of God with my covenant prayer partner. He was all the way in NY and I was in AL, but we would pray and prophesy over the phone. It started with me pushing him and birthing him out in some areas of ascending in prayer. Then he would get charged and push me in other areas. Then we pushed one another. Having a synonymous desperation and pursuit after God catapulted us into places we hadn't experienced even in Church. We would come out of prayer and compare notes with what the Lord spoke to both of us.

How: To eradicate the spirit of error there needs to be an apostolic alliance; a team of people who can: 1) Be **Ready** when God speaks, 2) **Aim** with precision and Kingdom direction, and 3) **Fire** with the potent power and glory of God! When an army arises with these kinds of strategies demonic kingdoms must come down. The *Giant Goliath* systems that are taunting our nations will be eradicated by the precision of Davidic Stones! Davidic Sounds of Praise! Davidic Sounds of Worship! Davidic Prayer and Intercession! Davidic Prophecies and Apostolic Strategies via God's Word! We must go the way of the Lord.

When: It took me until almost the age I am now to recognize God wanted me to chronicle my seasons of prayer. Every year is 3 Trimesters of Life for me. Three transitions take place throughout my year that I am still trying to master to this day. When I feel the transition happening I try to shift in my posture of prayer so that I am perfectly aligned with what the Father is speaking, and even requires me to speak.

Prayer Trimester – These are often very sensitive seasons where I feel God heavily. I get pulled to prayer regarding the slightest thing. I feel the stirring of God in my belly because He's troubling the waters for what He is about to say. As mentioned before, He is impregnating me. I spend lots of time in worship, praying in the Holy Ghost, and listening. This should not be a very talkative season.

Prophetic Trimester – During these months there is a bubbling up to speak. The Nabi anointing is coming forth. Nabi means to *bubble up*. Rivers of living water began to flow out and be spoken (John 7:38). What was deposited in the prayer season now springs forth (Isaiah 43:19) with prophetic decrees and declarations. These are seasons I am speaking to the winds to command change.

Apostolic Trimester – Then as I mentioned at the beginning of this chapter, there are times when it seems like God has become distant but he hasn't. A sobering now comes to carry out the instructions of the Lord. These are the times to build, administrate, analyze, re-evaluate, structure, realign, restore, launch, demonstrate, and even train via prayer modules and structures. It requires maturity in this place and season to also be the midwife to others and from a sober, mature place walk others through areas that have been conquered.

Who/What: Knowing who and what your adversary is during Apostolic Intercession will save and preserve you. I'm getting ready to share some testimonies of prayers, but as an example of the *who* and the *what*, there is a warning that I share concerning water contamination below. It took a while to realize I was not supposed to just pray against the water situation, but rather target Marine spirits that can get in the water supply and cause sickness to a nation of people. I'm getting ready to share this so that we will take note of how deep we must dig in prayer and who/what must be targeted to eradicate root systems. If I were to just say, "*Lord cleanse our water and protect us*", it does not speak to the spirit producing the polluted water in the seas. It can later resurface and cause a flood or other ongoing water issues. Everything concerning apostolic prayer must have a bullseye effect.

Testimonies of Apostolic Intercession

In January 2014, the Lord showed me a dream regarding the contamination of water in the United States. There was a live news report stating there was an urgency to conserve and salvage all clean and pure water. If the hydrant's water was clear, people were ordered to save it. If it was already a brownish color, they were ordered to try and go out to purchase as much water as possible because water supply would be cut off for an indefinite amount of time within the next 24-48 hours.

That dream did not reach the level of covering the U.S. instantly, but I believe it was shown in the form of severity to sound an alarm and charge people to take action. At least ten states were affected by polluted water, shortage of water, and massive water supply issues from 2014-to the present. It even took a severe turn for the worst the middle part of 2015 where even bottled water was being pulled off the shelves due to contamination being found in it.

Last year, January 2015, the Lord released a similar word regarding the contamination of food such as chicken, fish, beef and other food items. The Lord spoke to me to inform the people to go deep in prayer and to keep their lips close to His mouth, as there will be seasons that He will speak of particular foods to refrain from eating. We cannot depend on news reports. More likely than not, by the time it hits the news our bodies can already be infected. He spoke in depth about areas that must be strategically identified. While we have heard of, and come into the knowledge of marine spirits, various principalities, etc. the Lord said this is a time that we must ride out into the deep as intercessors and prayer warriors.

I was in prayer one night and the Lord said there are demonic spirits and entities that lurk in places that we refuse to go. We play it safe while many unknown attacks are launched out into the earth, as they remain in hidden places beyond the surfaces and perimeters of the earth. He said to strategically call them out! I could see demonic injections listed under foreign names, which causes familiar sicknesses such as various forms of cancer.

However, these are not eradicated until we call them out by name. Notice the so-called drugs, or discoveries, that are in our food have unknown foreign names? During prayer the Lord said He will begin to reveal specific names of ingredients that are laced in our food. I saw a vision of a submarine hitting the bottom of the ocean and gliding through unfamiliar territories of creatures. He said we must be able to use the necessary vehicle in prayer to travel into the abyss and eradicate our enemies. Everyone cannot travel countries in a car, crossing waters and lands. You must fuel up your jet in the spirit and move and shift and soar!

I am not a military expert, but I do know that when attacks are launched from other countries, we do not wait until they come to us. We send our troops to go and deal with the hidden problem. God began to say there are spirits that hide and lurk in our wilderness areas jungles, woods that infect our animals. There are princes and spirits of the air that extend to other planets, which is why we see and hear of so many "alien-like" attacks. Apostolic intercessors must launch our prayers and throw our voices like an arrow to declare perpetual victory over the earth.

Ephesians 6:12 (KJV) For we wrestle not against flesh and blood, but against principalities, against powers, against the rulers of the darkness of this world, against spiritual wickedness in high places.

Principalities are beginning to merge and lock arms, which is why we are seeing so much chaos multiplying, governmental chaos, political head-butting, businesses collapsing, and stock markets crashing. I had a dream recently about mixed breed animals. I looked outside and there was a giant iguana with the spots and skin of a python. When it stood up it was a full-blown beast that looked something like a T-Rex dinosaur, but it had the face of a dog. They represent beasts of power, ancient spirits, and principalities that seek to become the driving force for all 7 Mountains (business, education, government, media, family, religions, entertainment) to conquer our world.

The enemy is working overtime to wreak havoc in the earth. Therefore, we can't afford to move in error, hear in error, speak in error, or live in error. We cannot allow the Body of Christ to function with a Breeched Seed. Satan desires to sift us as wheat and cause everything we have labored, prayed, and worked so hard for to be delayed and denied because of a breeched posture. We cannot allow the enemy to turn our seed in the wrong direction.

If our posture is prayer, we cannot be shifted, distracted, or entertained by anything that does not reflect God's plan. As a Church when the Lord is preparing His headship, His generals, His supremacy to go forth and release His Word to those in high places, He should not see the feet preceding the head.

Prophetic/Apostolic Insert

I hate to go back to this, but I hear the Father saying, *"There is a premature army that has risen! Under-developed, haughty, high-minded, unsubmitted, and flowing in error. Your feet have not been planted to the foundations of My Word and Prayer! As the babies that are breeched, improperly cradled in the womb, so have you been improperly cradled in your ministries. Millennials you are coming out as an exceeding Great Army, but you are an Army with no strategy! You are an Army with no wisdom! You are an Army with no insight! You are an Army with no stability! You are Armed with no Aim! You are an Army with no covering! You have zeal, but no knowledge* (Romans 10:2). *You are accurate, gifted, sharp, astute, intellectual, and voguish. Yet you lack purity, brokenness, and obedience.*

You have become quality show-offs that attempt to belittle and grandstand those who have invested in you to build you. You have become impressed with your own skills, talents, gifts, and style; superseding those who have paved the way before you. They have become tired and weary. You are young, fast, strong, and vibrant. Your gifts are bright, shiny, and attractive. My intended purpose was for each generation to assist one another

(Genesis 25:23). *I called the young because you are strong and can carry on the legacies of the fathers, Prophets! I called the old because they know the way and shall direct your feeble minds of arrogance and erroneous revelations (I John 2:13 – 14).*

IF you will repent and allow me to perform a divine TURNING in you there shall be breakthrough and deliverance in the land. Malachi 4:6 says, "And he shall TURN the heart of the fathers to the children, and the heart of the children to their fathers, lest I come and smite the earth with a curse. THE END OF THE PROPHETS." The TURNING I am speaking of in this hour is to eradicate the BREECH of GENERATIONS! Your blessing and birthright is still in the hands of your fathers, leaders, and those who have the authority to bless or curse you because of your disobedience. You have stained your birthrights with blood guiltiness, but I will restore you and heal you. I will launch you back into paths of righteousness; divine wealth and health if you will harken to My voice! My plans for your Great Expected End still stands true if you will simply Align your will with Mine, says the spirit of the Living God!

My instructions are to tell the *dry bones* to Hear the word of the Lord. There are intercessors who pray countless hours, days, and even years in some churches or concerning certain matters. It seems like their prayers and words are ignored. You must command your atmosphere to open, to hear, and to receive the command of the Lord. Unstop the hearing of the atmosphere, the hearing of the nations, and the hearing of the earth with your mouth! Yes, the earth has ears! They were created in the book of Genesis and ALL CREATION was formed by the spoken word of the Lord (Genesis 1st Chapter). The Bible says in Mark 4:41 as they were riding through the storm Jesus spoke to the winds, "Peace, be still." They asked, "What manner of man is this that the winds obey him?"

Special Insert:
I want you all to understand I just encountered a divine moment. I paused right here because no sooner than I finished the ending of that paragraph (literally) I just got a notification beep on my phone and checked it. A woman of God messaged me via inbox on Facebook and said:
"Your heart screams for the world to wake up to the living God, but every time He lays you on that floor and sends you deep past the veil, many more ears have become unglued. Your walk is going to get hard in the end days ...But your name is Victorious! They will hear you loudly and clearly."

I had to stop and ask her did she just say, "their ears have become unglued"? As in *unstop the hearing*? She said, "Yes!" She also did not know I had just gotten off the floor in my prayer room before I came out and started typing what I wrote above. While I was on the prayer room floor, I started looking through a journal where I kept sermons and prophetic words. One of the notes said, "Give Me Thy Ear Oh Zion!" I need you to understand that this is happening right now as I am typing this. This was not intended to be in the book, but apparently the Lord wanted emphasis right here on the **opening of the ear**!

I even hear the Lord saying, "Your ear gates are doorways to the unfolded mysteries of my Word. When I speak to you I am giving you access just as you have access when you come into a door) to new revelation! That revelation, that freshness, that prophetic breath and wind from your mouth will bring life to the *death* and *deaf* areas where you launch intercession.

We have to stand with the anointing of Ezekiel and prophesy and breathe into the army of dry bones that surround us through prayer and intercession. We have to speak to the winds of our climate and our atmospheres. There were specific instructions given to Ezekiel. What was visible before him looked hopeless, lifeless, and purposeless. However, the Lord spoke to him in Ezekiel 37 and there were several instructions and strategies in the spoken word from God. The first thing spoken was Prophesy!

Next, the Lord gives specificity to what Ezekiel needed to prophesy! He says in Ezekiel 37:5-6, "I will cause breath to enter into you, and ye shall live: And I will lay sinews upon you, and will bring up flesh upon you, and cover you with skin, and put breath in you, and ye shall live; and ye shall know that I *am* the LORD." This is not only a prophetic command, but this is an apostolic demand. Not only as intercessors do we have to speak to a spirit, or to an atmosphere, but we must take full authority and declare how it shall take place according to the will of the Father. Leave no table unturned. Do not give the enemy any leeway to function as he desires.

Ezekiel obeyed and there was a noise, a shaking, and movement because the bones came together. Let me pause here again, please understand why intercessors and prophetic people are not moved by noise, shaking, and movement *alone*. Too often, we come to church and what should be a sound is nothing more than noise. People shake, rattle, and role. Yet the intercessor is not moved...but rather aggravated. Why? The Bible tells us he was given more instructions to now Prophesy to the winds (verse 9).

The spirit of religion would be happy with just the shaking because it looks like results. Intercessors will drive through the obstacles and opposition until they see results manifest. The Bible says after the sinews and skin came on them there was no breath in them. There was no life! How were they moving and shaking and coming together, but there was no life? So, he was told to breathe into them. Life enters into them and they stood up an exceeding great army (verse 10).

What you must remember is what you breathe into will raise up a nation. What you breathe into will cause an army to arise. Whom you impart into and whom you birth out in prayer will arise in mass multitudes. Give your ear to God intercessors! He cannot use your mouth until He first has your ear. Then as He did when He spoke to Elijah in a whisper, sometimes He will purposefully speak softly to see how close you are.

The Lord spoke to me about something once, but He said it so light I missed it. I said, "God why did you speak in such a faint voice about something so serious?" He said to me immediately, "If My voice is too faint…It's because you are too far!" Our ears should be to His mouth, as an umbilical cord is connected from a baby to the mother. It gives oxygen and provides nourishment just as the Word of God does when we are connected to Him. Don't miss the details of God's Deposits!

Chapter Five
The Crowning of Purpose

"Contractions sound the alarm for the delivery of your promise."

As contractions continue, you start to master timing and know when another one is on the way. You brace for the pain. At this phase, the normal panting, breathing, and even the common push is not enough to get through this last leg of delivery. Contractions come to alarm the closeness of the delivery. Let that penetrate. *Contractions sound the alarm for the delivery of your promise!*

The sensitivity of intercessors are being heightened in the realm of the spirit. Intercessors, Prophets, Apostles, Pastors, Teachers, Leaders of any sort must be apt to discover the times and seasons as the sons of Issachar (1Chronicles 12:32). We must know what is upon us and how to posture with strategy. Often the greatest time of pain and weariness and tiredness is during the crowning. The baby is practically out, but the doctor always says, "I need you to give it one more PUSH to enjoy this new baby boy or girl."

While discovering the depths of ministry, supernatural

realms, and dimensions, most times we realize the weight of what we really carry. Though I have not dealt with this much throughout this book, I will slide in some hints of demonic warfare often faced in this place. Because the enemy does not like order, he uses the complication of confusion to divert the pathway of your seed.

This is why as an apostolic intercessor there must be strategy, there must be precision, and there must be an accurate focus according to the Word and Will of the Lord. One must not become anxious or desperate in this stage of delivery due to the timeframe of waiting. The extent of labor, carrying, and simply the anticipation or trust in erroneous voices of instruction can delay, not only the "ability to bring forth", but the "strength to bring forth" in your due season.

Isaiah 37:3 (NLT) *They told him, "This is what King Hezekiah says: Today is a day of trouble, insults, and disgrace. It is like when a child is ready to be born, but the mother has no strength to deliver the baby.*

The Lord reminded me of the last stages of pregnancy! Even Pregnancy Exhaustion! Prophetic Fatigue! Moreover, the Father said there are seasons where you have to be held in position during delivery because your body has literally given out! You need strong teams, leaders, voices of instruction to hold you up in prayer during exhausting seasons, after laborious assignments of pressing and warring.

A woman of God from Florida shared a powerful story with me years ago about the birth of her grandchild. The medical staff had to hold the mother (her daughter) in position to deliver her baby because she had been in labor for over 24 hours and each time the baby would get ready to come, she would pass out and the baby would go back up. Therefore, they *held her in* position to birth!

Who is holding you in your posture of power and strength during your seasons of fatigue? God took me back to the dream I mentioned earlier. He said it's not that there was anything demonic in your room, but watch who is covering you and surrounding you. Watch who is covering you during your seasons of fatigue. Be careful of who sees you in your down state and when warfare has gotten the best of you. Again, I say in prophetic warning, Be Careful Who is on Your Watch! Be careful when and where you let down your guard. Discernment is a key ingredient for every trimester.

Ezra 4:4   Then the peoples around them set out to discourage the people of Judah and make them afraid to go on building.

Nehemiah 4:20-23 (NLT)   When you hear the blast of the trumpet, rush to wherever it is sounding. Then our God will fight for us!" We worked early and late, from sunrise to sunset. And half the men were always on guard. I also told everyone living outside the walls to stay in Jerusalem. That way they and their servants could help with guard duty at night and work during the day. During this time, none of us—not I, nor my relatives, nor my servants, nor the guards who were with me—ever took off our clothes. We carried our weapons with us at all times, even when we went for water.

During apostolic operation, it consists of a time to build, govern, and set order. This is the hour that you must be aware of the times and the seasons (trimesters) of your delivery. Be sober and alert! Know what trimester of prayer is necessary for each circumstance. Remember you are now counting the contractions to see how far apart they are.

Again, pay close attention and chronicle the changes of your postures to pray. Count down and prepare according to shift according to God's calendar whether to *Push, Strategize, or Rest.* Journal and take note of the attacks that come during those trimesters of prayer so you can better brace yourself and gird up in fasting and prayer. Journal the symptoms such as increased dreams, visions, tears, repentance, or downloads of information.

I hear this in the spirit. Be sensitive to hours of evangelistic outpour. There are times that the floodgates are open for souls to be saved. Keep an eye on those even in your congregation who may be wrestling with giving their life to the Lord. Pay close attention to fidgety mannerisms. Alert your ministry's prayer team to be prepared to ask to pray with those individuals they feel led to during worship services. Of course, make sure this is approved and cleared by leadership.

However, I have seen the power of God fall in a service at inopportune times and an altar call breaks out during praise and worship, intercessory prayer, etc. and tons of people give their lives to the Lord under that open window of glory. This is why we cannot be locked into systems of religion and control in the Body of Christ. Gatekeepers keep targeting for free-flowing climates! Keep praying for combustible glory cultures!

Once you learn the functions of your trimester, even if God switches up on you and pushes you to apostolic intercession in a season that is typically prophetic, you will know it means to get in your apostolic posture. Prepare to engage in the delivery of God's orders. Be in sync with the Father. Operate on His time zone. There may be a shift in the earth realm, a shift in the second dimension, or a shift in the heavens. There may not be time to go through all of the prophetic techniques you are accustomed to. Rather there is a demand to function in apostolic agility.

We are in that hour! Again, the shock factor of Donald Trump winning the presidential election of 2016 sent a wave over the nation that shocked us out of the confines of normality. I believe it was one of the foolish gestures of God's mind to confound wisdom back to His people.

1 Corinthians 1:27 (NIV) But God chose the foolish things of the world to shame the wise; God chose the weak things of the world to shame the strong.

It shocked the Church back to prayer! It shocked the nation into an awareness of just how much our world is changing and needs Christ. We must be ahead of the game intercessors, and aware of the things that is upon us. Nothing surprises the Father, and if we function with Him it won't surprise us either.

With that being said, consider the state of our government. Look at the escalating number of earthquakes, hurricanes, mass murders, chaos and perversion in the Church. Discouragement attempts to overtake those who can bring strategy and direction to those with a *heart* and *ear* to hear what the Spirit is saying to the Church. Apostolic intercessors guard the territory of the Kingdom. Yet there are seasons that the enemy sends conflicting information and doubt to discourage the momentum of delivery in prayer.

Prayer is a building process. The Bible tells us to build ourselves up on our most holy faith, praying in the Holy Ghost (Jude 1:20). Just as the information has been building throughout this book, what increases our momentum and faith to continue the work of prayer and finish strong is when we see results.

No matter how tired or weary a woman is that is birthing a child, I believe that each time the physician tells her to just give it one more push, she trusts that it is the sacrifice of the last push that is going to deliver her victory. The fact that someone is watching and though you can't see what's going on while you are birthing as the mother, when they tell you that they can see the head there is an excitement and another wind of strength that comes upon you. Zion must put on its strength now and know that the head of glory is already out. The head of triumph is already out. The head of power is already out.

This revelation must be digested by every individual reading this book. Your purpose is the exact DNA to someone else's calling and anointing. Before we rejoice and wrap our baby, our seed, our ministry, our gifts in swaddling clothes and return to life to enjoy what we have birthed we must understand that much of what we birth is not for us, but someone else.

Many people have watched the movie, *The Color Purple*. At the very beginning, the main character, Celie, is birthing a baby that her father comes and takes out of her hands immediately. Though she is the mother, it is years before she sees or hears about the success of what she birthed. Often times, we deliver and we minister and we look for immediate results, or we want to be the one to raise the baby and show it off that it is ours.

There is no time to get accolades for what you birth in this hour. There is swift maturity required because of the times in which we live. No sooner than we deliver, we must get ready to pass that gift on by imparting, training, developing, and strategizing with others who need what is in us and prepare to be impregnated and birth all over again. Why? Because there is a need for the army of the Lord to be multiplied by the thousands.

Be prepared to be a Midwife, or even a Surrogate to those who cannot birth for themselves yet. This is why we labor as Trailblazers of Intercession; so that others won't have to go through the difficulty that we have. It is why I am telling the testimonies of things I have faced, things I did wrong, and ways I was done wrong. At the end of the day it is not about us. We have Purpose to Birth!

The final push is upon us! Though we are screaming out in travail, there is a promise upon us for greater. Your gift is crowning right before your eyes. Don't despise the pain, the baby is crowning! Breathe! God is in full control. Squeeze His hand. He's coaching you, directing you, and encouraging the power that is being delivered through you. Get ready for the final push of your trimester. Get ready to deliver the totality of your dreams, your goals, your vision, your business, your ministry! Don't mind the blood, the afterbirth, and all that the promise is covered with. It is yours! It is here!

Post Delivery

"Birth It...And Raise It!"

I remember years ago after I talked and preached about birthing for so long, the Lord finally spoke to me and said "Birth It and Raise It." There comes a time that we must move on from elementary doctrines and on to perfection according to Hebrews 6:1. Just as a baby can't remain in the womb forever, neither can what He has placed on the inside of you.

While birthing can be a beautiful process, it can also be a process that seems disgusting to the natural eye. Take for instance when the doctor places the newborn baby on the mother before cleaning. Many studies say that it is important for the baby to have that immediate bond with the mother with all of the placenta, blood, and jelly-like substances still on the baby. Yet the mother holds it, kisses it, and cries because of the joy of a completed process.

One day, the Lord allowed me to experience that in the spirit as I began the process of birthing out yet another individual through their deliverance. I knew their life was not yet clean, but they wanted God. I knew they still struggled with cursing and other strongholds, but I could feel the warmth and smell; the unique scent of afterbirth on them. Many experience that who may be evangelists reading this book. Those of you who are called to outreach, you have to be prepared to deal with natural odors, or smells from the homeless. Yet it is the most humbling experience to have someone cry in your arms as they receive Christ. Their smells and lack of cleanliness is not a factor. The new scent of their souls being saved is perfume to your nostrils, and so it is to God's.

The Lord said to me at that point "birth them and clean them". He said, "Too often we try to clean the baby before it is even two seconds out of the womb." He showed me the generation that He would have me to mother and minister to and love. He vowed to show me when to be strong with them, but by way of love and compassion. Walk out your process of maturity quickly intercessors, midwives, ministry leaders, and mentors. A nation awaits you with open mouths waiting to be fed.

For those who have been battling the call to train in intercession, or five-fold ministry, and you have been procrastinating and stagnant because of fear, bind that spirit and shake it out of your very being. The world is waiting on you. There are silent cries all over this nation from people who need to hear what you have been carrying silently for years. Intercessors get those books written and birthed out so that other intercessors may live because of the truth of your testimony and experiences. Prophets tell the raw story of your making! Apostles get those manuals out so that those coming behind you will have a map of Kingdom Guidance. Prepare the grounds of your ministries for Apostolic Succession. You must know this day that this generation needs us as midwives and surrogates to help them first understand their gifts and callings. Then they need to know how to walk it out in purity, submission, and maturity.

If your leader is not fathering you, pray for the transition from instructor to father. Not to leave, but pray for the burden of the Lord's heart (the Spirit of Abba) to rest upon him/her to begin to bond with their sheep. Pray that God teaches them how to father you through Him. Pray that God positions you, breaks you, humbles you to be the son and the daughter that is postured submissively as a teachable student to learn and receive.

Then pray that God sends someone to father them and show them how to father you and others. Do you know how many leaders just do not know how to father, train, develop, and raise the seeds even *they* have birthed? It's one thing to *Birth It!* It's another thing to *Raise It!* That's a lifetime process that seems overwhelming for some. Pray in general for all leaders that after they have done the will of the Father and raised their sons and daughters well, that they can simply *let go*.

Just as difficult as it is to take that teenager and drop them off at college for the purpose of higher learning, so is the need to raise sons and daughters as far as they can be taken under one leader's tutelage. One plants, another waters, but God brings the increase (1Corinthians 3:6-7). There must be more room made in the womb for other sons and daughters to receive the same amazing instructions and teaching that was given to others. Pastor, Bishop, Apostle, Teacher...you did well! You raised them and showed them the way to go, now trust your impartation and start on the next generation. There's nations inside of you that must come forth. The cycle begins again. Keep pouring. Keep Training. Keep Reproducing.

Destiny is calling each of you to become pregnant with purpose, carry it forth to full fruition, and deliver it in the earth to build a nation, the kingdom of God in the earth, as it is in heaven. God wants to migrate the heavens into the earth by using His mouthpieces through the vehicle of prayer and intercession. Whether you have identified your trimester of prayer as a general intercessor, a prophetic intercessor, and/or an apostolic intercessor your sound must be heard and released! Congratulations on the delivery of your Promise!

May the peace, presence, and power of God dwell with you now and forever; even until the end of time.

ENDNOTES

Quickening, Sex and Other Pregnancy Things. (n.d.). Retrieved March/April, 2016, from http://www.webmd.com/baby/features/when-feel-baby-move

Strong's Hebrew: 2421. חָיָה (chayah) -- live. (n.d.). Retrieved March/April, 2016, from http://biblehub.com/hebrew/2421.htm

Full Definition of Travel. (n.d.). Retrieved March/April, 2016, from http://www.merriam-webster.com/dictionary/travel

Breech Birth. (n.d.). Retrieved March/April, 2016, from http://www.babycenter.com/0_breech-birth_158.bc

About the Author

Melissa S. Sanders is a leading prophetic voice that has been called to The Emerging Church. She was birthed out by prophetic and apostolic leaders who were far beyond their years and allowed her the grace to bridge the gap of generations. She is known across the nations as "*The Prophetic Midwife*" - one who births the heart and will of God in the earth through His people by much prayer and travail. She is young in age, but mature and experienced in spirit. Her local ministry group, Empowering a Kingdom Generation, also known as E.K.G. exists to birth the heart of God and fulfill His mandate in its entirety. Melissa is an ordained Prophet and resides in Birmingham, Alabama where she is active in her ministry and community.

Booking info: ThreeTrimesters@yahoo.com

Facebook: Melissa S Sanders, M.A.

For additional Orders: Submit $20 to PayPal.me/3Trimesters

Made in the USA
Las Vegas, NV
20 August 2021